Compendium of
Sewing
Techniques

250 tips, techniques and trade secrets

Compendium of
Sewing
Techniques

250 tips, techniques and trade secrets

Lorna Knight

Search Press

COMPENDIUM OF SEWING
TECHNIQUES.

Copyright © 2010 by Quarto Inc.

Published in 2010 by
Search Press Ltd
Wellwood
North Farm Road
Tunbridge Wells
Kent TN2 3DR

Reprinted 2010, 2011

Conceived, designed, and
produced by
Quarto Publishing plc
The Old Brewery
6 Blundell Street
London N7 9BH

QUAR.STTS
ISBN: 978-1-84448-525-3

Project editor: Chloe Todd Fordham
Art editor: Jacqueline Palmer
Designer: Elizabeth Healey
Illustrator: Kuo Kang Chen
Photographer: Simon Pask
Design assistant: Saffron Stocker
Copy editor: Sally MacEachern
Proofreader: Helen Atkinson
Art director: Caroline Guest
Creative director: Moira Clinch
Publisher: Paul Carslake

Colour reproduction by
PICA Digital Pte Ltd, Singapore
Printed in China by
1010 Printing International Ltd

Contents

Introduction

 The world of sewing covers a huge range of skills encompassing clothes-making, soft furnishings, upholstery, patchwork, quilting, embroidery, crafts and even mending. Whether you are new to sewing, or you consider it to be your life and work, you can never have enough sewing knowledge. Even if you only sew when you have to – when a button falls off or a hem needs to be repaired – there are always little tips to learn to make the processes easier.

Sewing is a skill acquired with decades of practice. Tiny pieces of knowledge build together over the years to establish a thorough understanding and expertise. New and innovative products are constantly being developed to make tasks easier and allow a better finish to be achieved. It is essential to keep up to date with these advances and to introduce them into your sewing habits.

Whether you consider sewing to be your hobby or your profession, this book is intended to help you on your way. It gives those extra little snippets of information you need to achieve the finish you strive for. It will speed up your work and inspire you to try new techniques or creative effects.

This book is everything you need, in one volume, to make your sewing projects quicker and easier to make with a perfect, professional finish.

Lorna

About this book

The information in this book is presented in five chapters that will take you through everything you need to know about sewing, from using the right tools and materials, to finishing tips for neat, professional results – or you can dip in for help with a particular problem.

Tools and equipment
This chapter presents an overview on sewing basics, from needle know-how to troubleshooting for sewing machines.

Material matters
Selecting the right fabric for the right project can be difficult. This chapter is devoted to 'material matters' – sourcing, storing and sewing – and all those essential design choices.

In stitches
Whether sewing by hand or by machine, and whether your stitches are functional or decorative, this section will teach you all you need to know to get stitching.

Sewing techniques
There is so much you can do with a needle and thread. From joining fabrics to luxury linings, there's something in this chapter for everyone, regardless of your sewing skill level.

Decorating fabrics
This chapter offers inspiration on ways to embellish garments and soft furnishing projects, with myriad 'how to' tips and 'make it' suggestions.

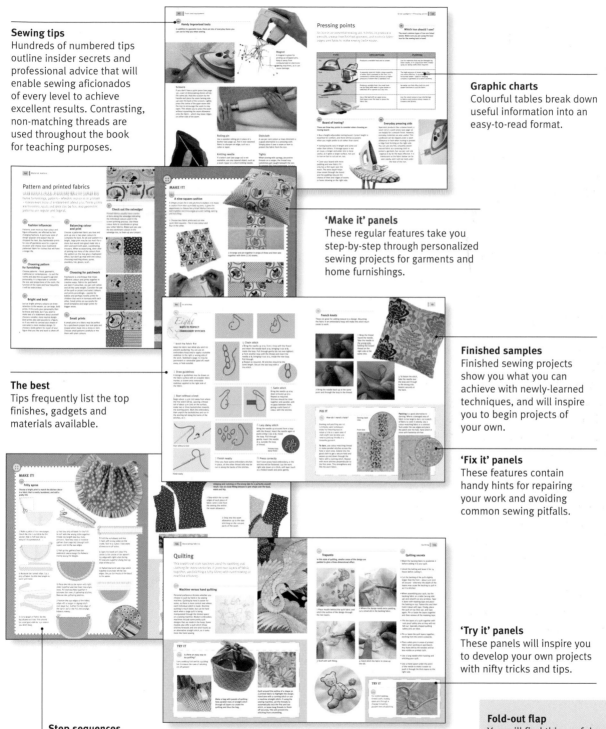

Sewing tips
Hundreds of numbered tips outline insider secrets and professional advice that will enable sewing aficionados of every level to achieve excellent results. Contrasting, non-matching threads are used throughout the book for teaching purposes.

Graphic charts
Colourful tables break down useful information into an easy-to-read format.

'Make it' panels
These regular features take you step-by-step through personalized sewing projects for garments and home furnishings.

The best
Tips frequently list the top finishes, gadgets and materials available.

Finished samples
Finished sewing projects show you what you can achieve with newly-learned techniques, and will inspire you to begin projects of your own.

'Fix it' panels
These features contain handy hints for repairing your work and avoiding common sewing pitfalls.

'Try it' panels
These panels will inspire you to develop your own projects with nifty tricks and tips.

Step sequences
A combination of full-colour photography and graphics teach you the basic sewing techniques in easy-to-follow sequences. Any difficult stitching is reiterated in a detailed close-up or diagram, helping you to achieve professional results.

Fold-out flap
You will find this useful pull-out page at the back of the book. On the flap there are details of stitch length conversions and an imperial to metric conversion chart for seams and hems.

Tools and equipment

As with any craft, it is so much easier to complete a task
if the right tools are on hand. Whether you are cutting
fabric, paper patterns or threads, there are appropriate
scissors for each case. The same applies to needles,
pins and those more obscure gadgets that speed up the
process and improve the finish. Use this chapter to select
the necessary tools to help with your sewing projects.

Essential equipment

As with any craft, specialist tools help to achieve a good result. While a needle is the minimum requirement, there are numerous useful tools, gadgets and materials that can make a sewer's life easier.

1

Nine

THINGS A SEWING ROOM CAN'T BE WITHOUT

1 Needles

Needles of various sizes are used for all sorts of tasks, from invisible hand sewing and embroidery to basic machine stitching and decorative machine effects.

2 Pins

Pins hold fabric in place before basting and stitching. Craft pins are suitable for many projects, while longer, finer pins are better for delicate fabrics. Use safety pins for threading elastic and cords through channels or for holding layers together when quilting. If you tend to lose or drop pins on the floor, buy ones with large pearl or beaded heads so you can find them more easily.

3 Measuring tapes

These are necessary for accurate working and making sure that dresses and trousers fit the wearer perfectly. Their pliability makes them ideal for measuring curves. When placed on an edge, a measuring tape can follow lines to give accurate sizing. Use a metal retractable measure for curtains.

4 Scissors

Scissors are essential for sewing. Use long-bladed shears for cutting out fabric and smaller, sharp-pointed needlework or embroidery scissors for snipping threads. Paper scissors are also a must for cutting patterns and templates, as dressmaker's shears will blunt when used for paper or card.

5 Ruler

Use a 15cm (6in) ruler for measuring shorter lengths like hem and seam allowances. It is easier to manipulate than a long tape measure or a 30cm (12in) ruler. A clear plastic ruler is ideal as you can see the fabric beneath it.

6 Iron

An iron is a vital part of a sewing room's equipment. Use it to open seams, press hems, and create folds and creases. An iron can often reduce the amount of pinning or basting between steps of a project. It also improves the finish of a piece of clothing, sharpening edges, smoothing creases and reducing bulk.

7 Seam ripper

This small tool is shaped to make it easier to undo stitches sewn in the wrong place. They vary in size but choose one that fits comfortably into the hand.

8 Work surface

A flat surface at a workable height, such as a table or worktop, is a fundamental part of a sewing room. Although you can cover the floor with a sheet before laying fabric over it for cutting out, most work needs a handy surface to prevent your knees and back from aching.

9 Sewing machine

Your sewing machine need not be the latest in sewing machine technology but it must be reliable and provide the functions you need. Look after it, keep it lint and dust free, and have it serviced regularly.

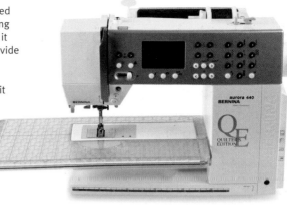

2

Five
USEFUL EXTRAS

There are some tools that may seem like luxury items, but after you've used them you will not be able to understand how you managed to sew without them.

1 Tailor's dummy

Set to the correct height and measurements, this can save time and make pinning, fitting and hemming much easier.

2 Tank iron

A tank iron holds a large reservoir of water that is converted to boosts of steam when needed. The power of the steam is greater than that of an ordinary iron and it does not require refilling so frequently. It also provides horizontal steam so it can be used for curtains hung on rails and garments on a tailor's dummy.

3 Serger

These useful machines (see page 27) are for neatening raw edges and giving clothes a professional finish. However, they also perform many other decorative functions and, although not essential, are a great asset.

4 Cabinet storage

Storage is a problem for people who sew. Growing collections of fabric, threads and patterns, together with books and equipment, must be housed and retrieved when needed. Special cabinets holding sewing machines are very useful, as are drawers, shelving and cupboards.

5 Pinking shears

Use a sharp pair of pinking shears to cut fabric and prevent it from fraying, or use on interfacing to soften its edge before ironing. Pinking shears are handy for craft projects, too.

Needle know-how

The needle is the principal piece of sewing equipment – you must have one if you want to sew! Originally whittled from bone or wood, needles are now made from high quality steel in sizes for every application.

Store used needles in a labelled cushion so they can be used again.

3

Anatomy of a needle

Hand needles

Hand needles come in a range of types and sizes to suit different tasks. Short fine needles are ideal for sewing small functional stitches, whereas larger eyed varieties are needed to take thicker embroidery threads. Keep a range to hand and select one most suited to your current project.

Eye

Body

Point

Groove: When the needle is in place, the groove faces forwards. The thread lies within it. This enables the needle to slip through the fabric, carrying the thread in the groove so it causes less drag.

Machine needles

Modern machine needles are adapted to suit particular fabrics and threads to give better results. The points vary, from sharp points that sew most fabrics without causing skipped stitches or damage to the fabric, to a rounded ball that slips between the yarns of knits without splitting them and wedged points for cutting through vinyl or leather.

Shaft

Scarf: The scarf is a hollowed area at the back of the needle. It allows the bobbin hook to grab the needle thread more easily to form a stitch.

Shaft

Eye

Point

4

Can't thread your needle?

- Cut the thread at an angle. This makes it easier to fit through the eye.

- Place a piece of white paper behind the eye of the needle to make it easier to see the hole for the thread to go through.

- Use a needle threading wire or gadget. There are many of these on the market (see below), ranging from a simple diamond-shaped wire on a handle, to tiny hooks that pull a thread length through the eye.

FIX IT

5 *Is your needle skipping stitches?*

- It is important to choose the correct machine needle for each task. It saves time and produces better stitches.

- Embroidery and metallic needles prevent the threads from breaking or shredding, which means that you don't have to keep rethreading the needle.

- If you need to change the type of needle while there is still some life in it, don't discard it. Make a needle cushion with segments for different sizes and types of needle. Write the information on the cushion with a fine permanent pen or embroider it by machine or hand.

- Use a magnifying glass to read the size on the body of the needle.

- Replace needles frequently; don't wait until they bend or break. As the needles dull, they will cause skipped stitches and may even damage the fabric.

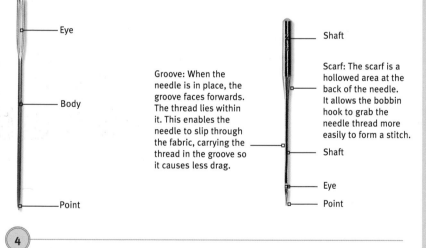

Flat wire hook for needle threading.

The diamond-shaped wire pulls thread through the eye of the needle.

A needle gadget makes threading easier.

MAKE IT!

Simple storage bags

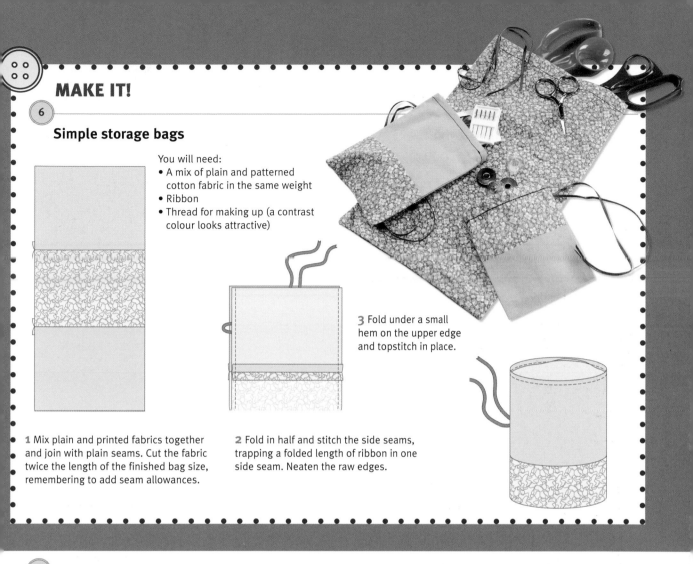

You will need:
- A mix of plain and patterned cotton fabric in the same weight
- Ribbon
- Thread for making up (a contrast colour looks attractive)

3 Fold under a small hem on the upper edge and topstitch in place.

1 Mix plain and printed fabrics together and join with plain seams. Cut the fabric twice the length of the finished bag size, remembering to add seam allowances.

2 Fold in half and stitch the side seams, trapping a folded length of ribbon in one side seam. Neaten the raw edges.

Threading your needle

One of the hardest tricks to learn when beginning to sew is how to thread small-eyed needles.

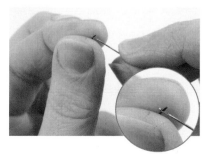

1 Don't bring your thread to the eye of your needle; bring the needle to the thread. Hold your thread with the sharply cut end sitting between your thumb and index finger on your non-dominant hand – hold it so you can barely see it. The more you can see of it, the more it is able to move and the harder it will be to thread.

2 Bring the eye of your needle down to the thread and push it onto it. This gives the thread the only option of going through the eye.

3 As soon as a piece of the thread is through the eye, you can continue to push – or pull the rest of the thread through.

8

Choosing needles

It is important to select the correct needle for the task in hand whether for hand sewing or machine sewing. Neat hand sewing is easier to produce with the correct size and type of needle and, although machine needles may all look the same, their subtle differences tailor them for particular threads or fabrics.

Hand Generally sizes range from 1 (largest) to 12 (finest)		
TYPE	**DESCRIPTION**	**PURPOSE**
Embroidery (crewel)	Medium length with a long eye to take embroidery threads.	Embroidery.
Beading	Long and very fine; thin enough to pass through the hole in a bead.	Beading.
Tapestry (chenille)	Blunt needle, shorter than a darner, with a large eye.	Tapestry, needlepoint and silk ribbon embroidery.
Bodkin	Long and broad with a rounded point and a large eye.	Threading elastic, ribbon or tapes through a casing.
Sharp	Medium length with a small round eye for general sewing.	General sewing projects.
Betweens	Shorter needles with a round eye.	Detailed, precise work for tailoring and quilting.
Darning	Long needle with a blunt end and large eye to take woollen yarn.	Darning.
Milliner's (straw)	Longer length with a round eye.	Basting, pleating and hat making.
Leather (glover's)	A sharp, wedged, triangular point to pierce leather.	Leather, suede, vinyl and other tough materials.

Machine
Sizes vary from 8 (fine) to 20 (large)

TYPE	DESCRIPTION	PURPOSE
Universal	Standard needle with a sharp point to penetrate most fabrics without causing damage.	Most weights of woven fabric.
Dullpoint	Rounded point to slide between the fibres rather than split them.	Knitted fabrics or those with spandex.
Stretch	Deep scarf to prevent skipped stitches.	Stretch fabrics, including knits, spandex and synthetic suede.
Microtex	Sharp point for fine fabrics.	Delicate silks and synthetic microfibre fabrics.
Denim	Strong needle with a sharp point.	Denim and other strong fabrics with a dense texture.
Metallic	Large polished eye holds thread and prevents it from shredding and skipping stitches.	Metallic threads including monofilaments.
Embroidery	Larger eye holds the embroidery floss and scarf allows dense stitching without shredding the thread.	Rayon, polyester and specialist embroidery threads.
Quilting	Sharp point and narrow, tapered shaft.	Sewing through several thick layers without damaging them.
Topstitch	Very sharp with a larger groove to take thicker threads.	Topstitching.
Wing (hem stitch)	Wings on either side of the shaft push fabric threads apart; well-chosen stitches leave decorative holes in cloth.	Decorative heirloom stitching similar to hand-sewn thread work. (Iron fabric with spray starch for a stiffer finish before starting to sew.)
Twin (triple) needle	Two or three needles fixed to a single body for parallel rows of stitching.	Heirloom stitching, pin tucks and double topstitching.

Pin pointers

Pins are vital for preparing fabric to sew. Use them to secure a paper pattern to material for cutting out, to hold two pieces of fabric together in a mock seam to check the fit, or to hold pleats or hems in place before stitching. Whatever you use pins for, make sure they are sharp and rust-free.

6 Flower head pins

Large, flat heads make the pins secure in loosely woven fabrics, like lace, net and tulle.

9

Working with net or tulle

Use safety pins rather than standard straight pins when working with net or tulle. To divide a large section of net for gathering into a full underskirt, use safety pins to identify the sections as standard pins will fall out.

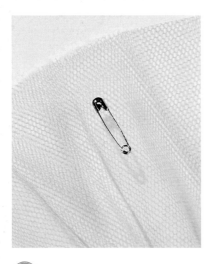

10

Perfect pins

1 Craft pins

Fairly thick, general purpose pins, for all kinds of projects.

2 Bridal pins

Bridal pins are long and fine to cause minimum damage to fabrics.

3 Dressmaker's pins

Finer and longer than craft pins, dressmaker's pins have larger glass or pearl heads and are easy to find when dropped.

4 Quilter's pins

Quilter's pins are long for use with thick layers of batting or fabrics such as synthetic furs.

5 Safety pins

Use safety pins when ordinary pins are likely to fall out (in net, for example) or if pins will remain in a project for some time (in quilt, for instance).

11

A weighty alternative

When pins cannot be used – the fabric may be too thick to penetrate or pinholes will permanently damage the material – weights are a good alternative. These might simply be kitchen weights or, for large soft furnishing projects, a brick in a woollen sock (see opposite page). Use the weights to prevent a paper pattern from moving when you cut out the fabric, as shown right.

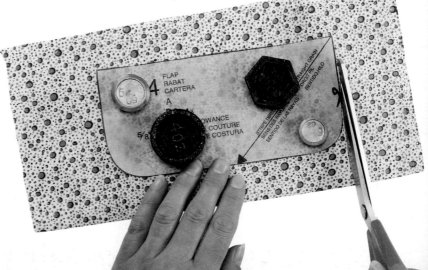

(12)

Transform a brick into a fabric weight

A large weight is useful for curtains and large soft furnishing projects. Add padding to the brick (as shown) to protect the fabric you are sewing. The handle makes it easy to move around.

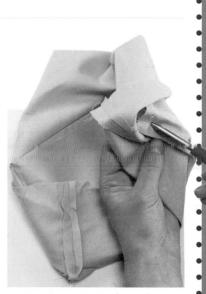

1 Wrap a brick with batting, like a parcel, and hand stitch to secure.

2 Measure the faces of the brick and add a seam allowance of 1.5cm (⅝in) to each edge. Choose a light-coloured fabric and cut out the pieces.

3 Pin and sew the shape together, leaving the base. Turn through.

4 To make the handle, cut a rectangle of fabric 45 x 12cm (18 x 4¾in). Sew with right sides together, turn through and press flat with the seam down the centre on the lower side. Pin and machine sew the ends of the handle to the centre of each side.

5 Slip the cover and handle over the brick. Turn over. Press the seam allowances of the fabric piece for the bottom to the wrong side and place this over the base of the brick. Pin and stitch by hand, securing all raw edges inside.

13

Top tips for pinning

- Discard all bent and rusty pins.

- Keep a box or container for old pins and needles. When it is full it can be thrown away safely.

- Some pins have large plastic heads. Do not iron over these, as they melt!

- Use small-headed craft pins when pattern making. Large-headed pins can distort measurements that are critical to achieving a perfect fit.

- Do not sew over pins. Even if pins are placed across the seam it is not safe to stitch over them, as pins and needles may break and shatter, throwing up tiny pieces of metal. Simply remove the pins as you reach them.

- Attach paper patterns to fabric with pins placed within the pattern boundary. In this way you will avoid cutting them with scissors. It might not be a problem to the pins but it may well damage the scissor blades. Also, when pinning delicate fabric, the body of the fabric can't be damaged when pinning within seams.

15

Pinning for beginners

If you have been sewing for years, pinning comes naturally. Beginners may find it more difficult. Simply put the pin through the fabric, then fold the fabric close to the point and bring the pin back to the surface.

14

Perfect your pinning technique

Everyone has their own preferences when pinning, but you will need to choose different methods for different tasks.

Pinning along the seam line

When pinning a garment together to check the fit of a skirt or whether a sleeve fits smoothly into an armhole, pin along the seam line like mock stitching. You can then check its appearance from the right side.

Pinning perpendicular to the seam line

Some tasks, such as sewing curtains or multiple layers of fabric, benefit from the pins being placed across the seam line so they can be easily removed as you reach them.

Great gadgets

Specialist gadgets and tools are available to make sewing tasks easier. Some of these are well known and easy to get hold of; others are more obscure, but make a real difference when tackling sewing problems. When you find something new, share it with your sewing friends.

16

Eight

GREAT GADGETS

1 Tailor's ham

This shaped, densely stuffed cushion sits under a garment taking up the shape to aid pressing. The ham is not a uniform shape so it can be turned to suit, for example, the contours of the bust of a jacket or the hip of a skirt, making it easier to iron or to achieve a smooth finish.

2 Sleeve board

A sleeve board is a handy accessory that enables you to slip a narrow sleeve over it and iron without creasing the lower side. Jacket sleeve seams can be ironed while the rest of the jacket hangs off the ironing board out of the way.

3 Point press and basher

A traditional hardwood tool with a large base and a narrow top tapering to a point, a point press and basher is designed to allow an enclosed seam to be pressed right up to the corner. Simply place the collar, lapel or any enclosed corner over the point and iron the seam open. The seam allowances will then lie flat inside and give a smoother finish when the garment is completed. The basher (base) comes in useful when pressing the front edge and collar of a tailored jacket. Steam the edge with an iron and then press the basher heavily over it to sharpen the edge for a professional finish.

Place the enclosed seam over the point so the iron can reach right to the corner.

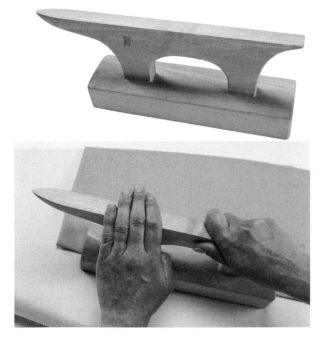

When the seam has been steamed, press with the basher to sharpen the edge.

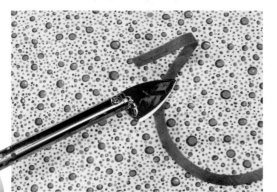

4 Tailor's awl

A small, tapered tool has a variety of uses. It helps turn corners and points through to the right side and can control fabric immediately in front of a sewing machine needle where fingers can't reach safely.

5 Mini iron

The small head of a mini iron can reach parts a standard iron cannot. It also irons only the area required and does not flatten or crease the surrounding fabric at the same time. It is useful when applying fusible bias tape or when pressing enclosed seams in conjunction with the point press.

A hook with latch is used to grab fabric and pull the tube through itself.

6 Bias-tape maker

This is great for making your own bias binding. Cut and join the bias strips and work on the ironing board. Use a pin to get the strip into the gadget and then feed it through, pressing the folded strip as it emerges at the opposite end. For best results, work with a natural fabric as it will hold the fold. Synthetic materials are more springy.

7 Tube turner

This simple wire makes turning narrow tubes of fabric so much easier. For button loops, shoestring straps or frog eye fastenings, the finest of cords can be produced. Make a small cut close to one end of the sewn tube. Slide the wire turner through from the opposite end and catch the cut loop with the hook. Make sure the latch encloses the loop and pull back, easing the tube through in the process. The raw edges do not need to be trimmed as they fill the tube, making it more of a round cord.

TRY IT

17 *Decorate plain fabric with a daisy foot*

Make a plain fabric more interesting with scattered daisies. Use the embellished fabric for a yoke (as shown) or cuffs, and the unsewn material for the rest of the garment.

8 Daisy foot

This presser foot attachment fits to most sewing machines and enables circular sewing to take place. Drop the feed dogs and set the sewing machine to a three-step zigzag. Adjust the daisy foot for the size of flower required and sew. With a little practice some beautiful effects can be created. Circular sewing attachments are available for many machines for sewing larger rings and around borders.

Bobby pin tube turner

If you do not have a dedicated tool to turn through a narrow tube, try this neat trick with a bobby pin. With a bit of practice, it is easy to make fine straps or button loops.

1 Cut a bias strip of fabric and stitch close to the fold, about 6mm (¼in). For added strength, sew a second row of stitching to reinforce the first. Make a snip 12mm (½in) from the end and slip the bobby pin into it.

2 Tuck the front end of the bobby pin into the tube and start to push. The folded end of the bobby pin will pull the end of the tube with it and then disappear into the tube.

3 Keep sliding the bobby pin through the tube, manipulating the fabric over itself in the process. Work with a small part at a time and do not let the creases build up or the bobby pin will get stuck.

4 Pull the bobby pin right to the opposite end and continue to work the folds and creases until the tube is fully through. The seam allowances sit inside the tube, filling it out and giving it a rounded shape.

Cardboard tube seam roll

Use a cardboard tube for pressing narrow sleeves and trouser legs. You will need: a long cardboard tube; an old clean wool blanket or a length of 100 per cent wool fabric and cotton sheeting.

1 Cut the tube to the length you need. Wrap just enough blanket around the tube to form a soft covering – one or two layers. Hand stitch the join and tuck the ends down into the tube.

2 Cut the sheeting or lawn to size and wrap it over the blanket. Tuck under the raw edge and slip stitch this to the lower layer. Tuck the ends under and sew a running stitch around each end. Tuck the raw edges to the inside and pull up the running stitches to neaten the ends.

20

Handy improvised tools

In addition to specialist tools, there are lots of everyday items you can use to help you when sewing.

Magnet

A magnet is great for picking up dropped pins. Keep it away from computerized or electronic sewing machines, as it can cause damage.

Scissors

If you don't have a point press (see page 19), a pair of dressmaking shears will do the same job. Hold the scissors by the handle and place the seam (wrong side up) over the back of the scissors. Lightly press the centre of the open seam with the iron to encourage the seam to stay open. This allows you to press the seam without squashing the seam allowance onto the fabric – which may leave ridges on either side of the seam.

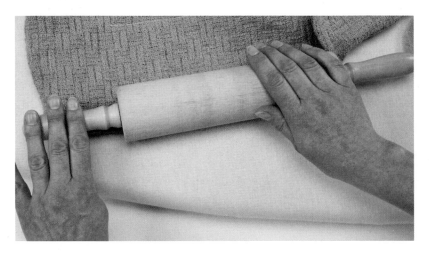

Rolling pin

Use a wooden rolling pin in place of a basher (see page 19). Roll it over steamed fabric to sharpen an edge, such as a collar or lapel.

Knitting needle

If a tailor's awl (see page 20) is not available, use any tapered object, such as a seam ripper or a short knitting needle.

Dishcloth

A 100 per cent cotton or linen dishcloth is a good alternative to a pressing cloth. Simply place it over a seam or hem to protect the fabric from the iron.

Tights

When sewing with springy, decorative threads on a serger, the thread may sometimes get caught beneath the reel. To prevent this from happening, cut up a pair of tights into lengths of about 15cm (6in) and slide a piece over the reel of thread. This holds the thread just close enough to stop it falling off and becoming stuck.

Pressing points

An iron is an essential sewing aid. It helps to produce a smooth, crease-free finished garment, and controls fabric edges and folds to make sewing tasks easier.

21 Which iron should I use?

The most common types of iron are listed below. Make sure you are using the best iron for the sewing task in hand.

TYPE	DESCRIPTION	PURPOSE
Dry	Produces a variable heat and no steam.	Use for materials that may be damaged by water marks, or in conjunction with a water spray (or damp cloth) when required.
Tank	A separate reservoir holds a large quantity of water that is pumped to the iron. It is converted to steam and produces a higher pressure of steam than a standard iron.	The high pressure of steam makes the iron more effective. It can also produce horizontal steam – ideal for hanging curtains or garments on a tailor's dummy.
Steam	Produces variable heat; the small tank can be filled with water to give steam or switched off to operate as a dry iron.	Versatile iron that offers both dry and steam functions to suit the fabric.
Steam press	Has a flat bed with an upper press that lowers over the base to press the fabric flat.	Use the steam press to fuse interfacings to fabrics and produce sharp creases in trousers and jackets.

22 Board of ironing?

There are three key points to consider when choosing an ironing board:

• Buy a height-adjustable ironing board. Correct height is essential for comfort, and there will be occasions when you might prefer to sit rather than stand.

• Ironing boards vary in length and some are wider than others. If storage space is not an issue, a longer and wider one is more useful, as it gives a larger surface, not just to iron on but to cut out on, too.

• Cover your board with more padding and new fabric if it only has a thin layer over the mesh. The extra depth helps draw steam through the board and the padding reduces the chance of lines and ridges of seams or hems showing on the right side.

23 Everyday pressing aids

Specialist products like a sleeve board, a seam roll or a point press (see page 19) are helpful for a smooth finish. However, everyday materials are also useful. Thin cardboard can be slipped under a seam allowance or hem when ironing to prevent a ridge from forming on the right side. You can use any fine, smoothly woven natural fabric as a pressing cloth to protect a garment, but 100 per cent silk organza is by far the most effective. It is translucent so the fabric below can be seen easily, and it will not melt under the heat of the iron.

Sewing machine tips

The sewing machine is your most important tool. It might not be the latest model, but it must be as reliable as a best friend, and should be treated as one. Never take it for granted, or it might let you down when you need it most!

24

Ten

CAN'T-DO-WITHOUT SEWING MACHINE FEET

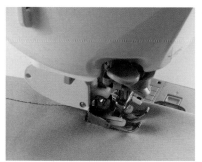

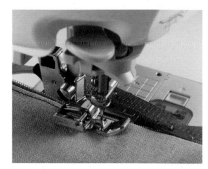

1 Straight stitch foot

Modern sewing machines have a large area within the feed dogs to take wide zigzag stitches. This is a really useful feature, but it can be a problem when working with fine fabrics, as there is a tendency for the fabric to be pushed down into the mechanism, damaging both fabric and machine. A straight stitch foot provides a small hole for straight stitching. This supports the fabric better and reduces the chance of it disappearing into the machine. A straight stitch plate is also available.

Warning: Make sure the machine is set to straight stitch, as the needle will break if it swings and hits the foot!

2 Walking foot

A walking foot is essential for anyone who does a lot of sewing and is well worth the investment. It walks over the fabric and prevents the upper fabric from sliding over the lower one. Use it for long seams on patterned curtains – to keep the pattern matching along the entire length – and for quilting projects where several layers are being sewn at once. Use it also to prevent knitted fabrics from stretching.

3 Zipper foot

A zipper foot allows stitches to be made close to the edge of the foot and is essential for putting in a zip neatly. It is also useful for piping, as the stitches can be positioned right at the base of the piping cord. An adjustable zipper foot is even more versatile as it can be moved to the exact position to suit your project.

4 Concealed zipper foot

Many skirts and dresses are now fitted with concealed zips, which are widely available in haberdashery shops. Their advantages are that an exact colour match is not essential and, when fitted, they are virtually invisible, looking like part of a seam. They are easy to insert, provided the correct foot is used. The feet vary in appearance from one machine to another, but work by twisting the teeth out of the way to allow stitches to be formed at the base of the teeth. A standard zipper foot will not sew close enough to the teeth.

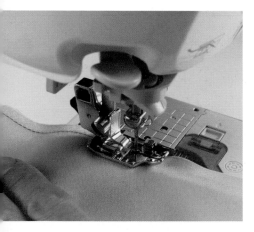

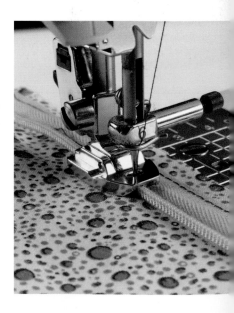

5 Open toe foot

This gives good access and visibility when sewing decorative stitching or appliqué. The stitches are not hidden by the foot as they are being formed and so it is easier to see the work. There is also a groove under the foot to allow a bulk of satin stitches to be formed without them bunching up.

6 Blind hemming foot

Blind hemming is a useful function on a sewing machine and, with the correct foot, the stitches are positioned perfectly. The foot has an adjustable guide, which feeds the folded fabric under the needle to allow just the right amount of fabric to be sewn. This forms a secure hem with no obvious stitches on the right side.

7 Darning/quilting foot

A darning or quilting foot is essential for quilting and machine embroidery. A small sprung foot that allows the work to be seen easily, it hovers over the work without putting pressure on the fabric.

8 Buttonhole foot

Buttonhole feet vary in style between makes and models but enable perfect buttonholes to be formed. Many automatic buttonholes can be made to the correct length of each button. Always practise making buttonholes on spare fabric before attempting it on a garment to check for possible problems. If there is no buttonhole foot, fit a presser foot suitable for decorative stitching and see page 66.

9 Pin tuck foot

Use this with twin needle tucks. As the rows of tucks are formed, subsequent rows are fed through the channels in the base of the presser foot, enabling perfectly parallel rows of tucks to be created. This is an essential foot for antique style sewing. Pin tuck feet with five and seven grooves are available.

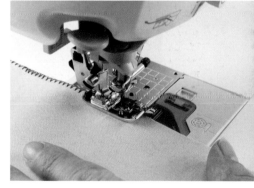

10 Overcasting foot

This is a very useful attachment for neatening raw edges. Place the cut fabric under the 'finger' guide and sew a zigzag or overcasting stitch along the edge. The stitches are formed over the 'finger' and then slide onto the fabric edge. With a standard foot, the stitches pull on the fabric edge, drawing it in, and do not produce such a neat finish.

Warning: Test the width of the stitch first to make sure the stitches are formed over the 'finger'. If the needle hits the foot it will break!

25 Carrying case

If you attend workshops and courses and have to take your sewing machine, invest in a proper carrying case. This makes it easier to transport and provides better protection for the sewing machine. If you transport your machine in the boot of your car, place it on a large piece of foam rubber to help soften the jolts.

26 Machine maintenance

- Service as required. This will depend on how frequently the machine is used. Follow the guidelines given in the manual or by the dealer.

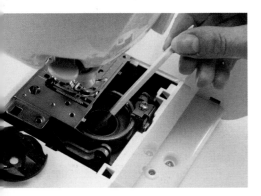

- Keep the machine dust and lint free. Use a small brush or cotton swab. Pressurized cans of air are a popular way to remove lint from a machine, but they may only be blowing the lint further into the mechanism, which will cause trouble at a later date.

- Many modern machines may not require lubrication. If this is the case, leave it to the mechanic when it is serviced.

- Cover your sewing machine when not in use. Dust seems to appear from nowhere and the machine's plastic casing may discolour in sunlight.

27 How to make a machine cover

Make a cover to protect your machine when it is not in use.

1 Measure the length, height and depth of the machine and add seam allowances to all sides.

2 Cut out one top, a front and back, and two sides. Decorate the front panel with a selection of the stitches from your machine before sewing the pieces together. Fold up a double hem at the bottom of the cover and topstitch in place. It is good to see the stitches rather than look at diagrams of them in the sewing machine manual.

28 Buying a machine

Research

If you have decided to invest in a new sewing machine, do as much research as possible before you commit yourself to a particular make or model. Ask friends about their machines, attend sewing exhibitions and visit sewing machine retailers to ask their advice.

Types of sewing

What sewing do you enjoy, and are you looking to do something different in future? Whether you quilt, make clothes or curtains, or do machine embroidery, it will affect your choice of machine. Select a machine that will suit your needs and consider how you would like your sewing to develop. Do not restrict yourself or you will quickly grow out of your new machine.

Stitches

There will be certain stitches you know you will need. For example, you may require a good variety of buttonholes or a nice range of decorative stitches. Make sure the machine you choose includes what you require.

Try it out

When searching for a new machine, take some fabric with you. Try out different machines with the type of fabric you tend to use and see how it copes. Some models work better with delicate lingerie fabrics, while others are more suited to thick layers of quilting.

Local retailer

Carefully consider where you buy your machine. There may be a fantastic deal on the Internet but sales advice may not be easy to access. Your local dealer, however, will be there to help in the months and years to come, and will offer a far better service if you bought the machine from him at the outset.

Modern machines

You can sew well if you have a sewing machine, basic equipment and some useful gadgets, but there are some additional machines that make life even easier – or just more fun.

29

Five OF THE BEST MACHINES FOR SEWING

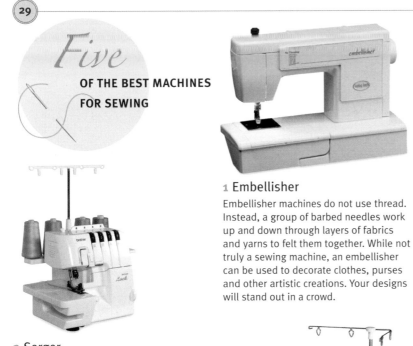

1 Embellisher

Embellisher machines do not use thread. Instead, a group of barbed needles work up and down through layers of fabrics and yarns to felt them together. While not truly a sewing machine, an embellisher can be used to decorate clothes, purses and other artistic creations. Your designs will stand out in a crowd.

2 Blind hemmer

This small machine hems invisibly and effortlessly. Use it for curtains as well as for cuff, trouser, and dress hems, especially if you are running a small business making clothes, soft furnishings or carrying out alterations.

3 Serger

For people who make clothes, a serger is almost an essential part of a sewing room, but for tailoring or quilting it might be considered an extravagance. A serger uses three or four threads and cuts, sews and neatens seams all in one. Use it to construct garments made from stretch fabrics and to neaten the raw edges of most other projects. If you are making clothes for other people or for fairs and bazaars, it produces a much more acceptable finish. It also sews a range of decorative effects and uses interesting threads and yarns. For more information on sergers, see pages 72–75.

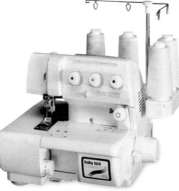

4 Coverstitch machine

Similar to a serger, a coverstitch machine goes even further, offering more decorative stitch options, a chain stitch and a cover stitch (sewn through fabric rather than on an edge). It uses up to eight cones of thread and can be complicated to thread at first. Use for sewing T-shirts and working with knit fabrics.

5 Fab-U-Motion

This quilter's aid allows smooth, free-motion sewing. With the help of a sensor, it regulates the speed and stitches to give a very neat result. The table glides with the quilt or embroidery for confident sewing.

Clever cutting

Blades of all shapes and sizes are available and each has a task to perform in the sewing room. Get the best results by using the right tool for each job.

30

Scissors stash

TYPE	DESCRIPTION	PURPOSE
Shears	Large scissors with long sharp blades and moulded handles for comfort.	Cutting fabric quickly with a smooth edge.
Pinking shears	Large scissors with notched blades giving a zigzag cut.	Giving a ravel-resistant edge to fabric in dressmaking and craftwork.
Needlework/ embroidery scissors	Small scissors with short blades and sharp points.	Cutting threads, difficult-to-access corners and unpicking stitches.
Serrated shears	The serrated blades hold fabric as they cut, stopping it from 'running away' from the blades.	Ideal for difficult-to-cut metallic, plastic, or novelty materials – or even silks and satins.
Curved embroidery scissors	Small, curved scissors with short blades and sharp points.	Cutting threads close to others; especially useful for machine embroidery.
Paper scissors	Medium-sized general-purpose scissors.	Cutting paper patterns and cardboard templates so that fabric shears can be kept for cloth alone and remain sharp.

TRY IT

31 *What's the best way to cut fur fabric?*

Cut fur fabric from the wrong side with small needlework scissors. Cut the backing only and then tease the fur apart. This reduces the need for a vacuum cleaner!

32

Alternative cutting tools

As well as using scissors to cut fabrics and threads, there are other cutting gadgets in the sewing room. They are useful additions to your sewing box and will save both time and energy.

Rotary cutter

This has a circular blade with a handle and is used with a self-healing mat placed under the fabric. It cuts fabric accurately and several layers can be cut at once. This makes it ideal for patchwork and small garment pieces. It is a fast method of cutting out. Here are a few useful tips:

• Buy two blades so there is always a spare if the other gets damaged.

• Buy the largest mat you have space for, especially if you are using it for clothes as well as patchwork.

• Keep the mat flat and away from heat, as it can bend and crack.

Buttonhole chisel

Opening buttonholes neatly without snipping the threads can be difficult – but not with a buttonhole chisel. Place over the centre of the buttonhole and tap the end to cut through the fabric.

Thread cutter

These handy little cutters hang around your neck so they can't get lost when you need them. The blade for cutting threads is concealed behind a disc with slots. The thread is cut by the blade when it is pulled into a slot.

Thread snips

Thread snips have no handles so they are easy to pick up quickly. Use them when sewing on the move and space for equipment is limited.

Seam ripper

A seam ripper cuts individual stitches when needed. The pointed end slips under the stitch and the sharp inside edge cuts the thread. They vary in size; choose a larger one for comfort, as it is easier to grip when undoing a long seam (see page 80).

Craft knife

A knife is occasionally the best tool for a sewing task. Cut stiff vinyl or leather with a craft knife rather than scissors, as a much neater cut is achieved. Keep the knife sharp. A blunt knife is more likely to cut you because you will be putting more pressure on the blade. A knife with a retractable blade will keep safely in your toolkit.

33

Looking after your cutters

• If you attend a class or sewing group with friends, tie a length of ribbon to the handle of your fabric shears to make yours stand out.

• Blades become dull through use. Sharpen them when they need it.

• Dropping scissors on the floor can knock them out of alignment. Place them in the centre of the table when not in use, not close to the edge.

• Keep scissors dry and out of damp conditions where they may rust.

Troubleshooting for machines

Sometimes you may be disappointed with your
sewing or the machine may not work as it should.
Such problems can usually be prevented – or easily
solved – when you know how.

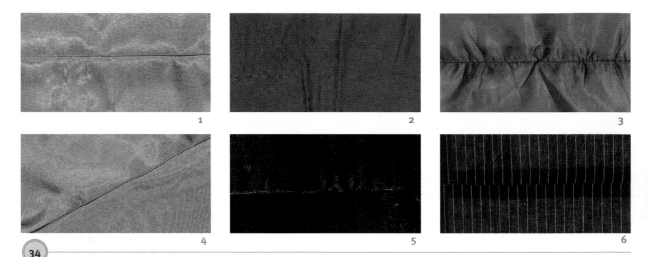

1 2 3
4 5 6

34

Fabric problems

1 Snagged fabrics

The usual cause of snags, often seen at a
seam, is a blunt or damaged needle.
Change to a new needle to remedy the
problem. Snags can also be caused by
using the wrong type of needle. Knits
require a ballpoint needle while
lightweight fabrics need a fine one. See
pages 14–15 for full details of needle
types and uses.

2 Puckering due to interfacing

When iron-on interfacing is not fused
properly puckering can occur. Modern
iron-on interfacings are woven or knitted
rather than being made from bonded
fibres. When in place, these move better
with the fabric and limit the chance of
puckering. Use a pressing cloth to protect
the fabric and interfacing. When fusing
interfacing to fabric, make sure both are
steam shrunk individually before placing
them together as they are likely to shrink
at different rates and cause dimples. Lift
and press the iron over the layers to cover
all areas and do not slide the iron over
the fabric until the layers are joined.
Allow to cool fully to prevent stretching.

3 Puckered seams

Long stitches or tight tension can cause
puckers along a seam. Shorten the stitch
length and loosen the needle tension to
see if this improves the seam. If the
problem remains, pull gently on the seam
in front of and behind the needle to
support the stitching while sewing. To
achieve a smooth join, iron the seam flat
first then open and iron the stitches from
the wrong side. Finally, hover the iron over
the surface of the seam lightly.

4 Bias seams

Sagging or stretching can occur when bias
fabrics are joined as it is difficult to
control the stretch of the off grain fabric.
Accurate cutting of pattern pieces is
essential; if the angle of the grain is
different on adjoining panels, sagging or
stretching will occur on one of the sides.
To prevent this on necklines or bust
seams, stay stitch the off grain or bias cut
edges. This is a stabilizing row of
stitching, just inside the seam allowance,
sewn through each single layer before
sewing the seam. For long straight bias
seams on skirts or dresses, pull gently
and evenly on the seam while sewing.

5 Shading variations

The nap or pile on the surface of a
fabric can cause differences in shading
to occur depending on how the light
catches it. For this reason, it is essential
that all panels of fabric are cut in the
same direction, otherwise shade
differences may be apparent. Velvet is
a good example of this.

6 Shifting fabrics

When sewing long seams of exactly the
same length there is often extra fabric
remaining on one side at the end of the
seam. This is due to the feed dogs that
move the fabric while the stitches are
made; the lower layer moves fractionally
more than the upper layer each time and
by the end of the seam this may result in
12mm (½in) difference. To reduce or
prevent this from happening, fit a walking
foot to the machine or hold the fabric of
the seam up by 90 degrees in front of the
presser foot rather than flat on the bed of
the machine. This helps to reduce the
upper layer shifting over the lower one.

35

Thread problems

If the top thread keeps breaking, it is probably not running smoothly through the thread guides.

- Check that it is unwinding evenly from the spool – it may be twisted around the spindle. This can happen if the spool moves up and down the spindle as you stitch. Add a spool (reel) cap (supplied with the machine) to keep the spool in place.

- Check that the spool is set the right way on the spindle. The thread should usually come over from the back to the front, but your sewing machine manual will show the correct direction for your type of machine.

- Do not use old thread, which can be weakened by age and break easily.

- Avoid using cheap thread, which can be uneven and prone to snap.

- A slight nick (invisible to the naked eye) in the eye of the needle can cause breaking thread. Nicks can result from the use of rough thread, such as metallic thread. Use a specially designed or large-eyed needle with such threads and insert a new needle for all other threads.

36

Machine jams

Removing lint: You should remove lint from the sewing machine after every project, and more frequently when sewing with fluffy fabrics, such as wools, fleece and knits. Take out the bobbin, blow out the lint and use the brush supplied in the accessories case.

Oiling: Modern machines are self-lubricating, but older models may need oiling. Check your sewing machine manual and follow the guidelines. Always sew scrap fabric after oiling to prevent surplus oil from damaging a project.

Buttonhole jam: Always reinforce the area to be stitched with interfacing to provide a good base for the concentrated stitching. Avoid stitching too close to the edge of the fabric – if the presser foot has insufficient fabric to grip, the fabric can be drawn down into the throat plate.

Foot pedal doesn't work: Check that the pedal is pushed firmly into the machine – it can work loose if the machine is moved. If the problem persists, ask your machine dealer to check the wiring.

No power: Check the plug and fuse. Make sure the wire is pushed firmly into the machine. Check that the bobbin-winding spindle is not engaged, preventing normal sewing. If the problem persists, contact your machine dealer and have the wiring checked.

37

Stitch problems

1 Skipped stitches: Skipped stitches are often caused by using the wrong needle for the type of fabric. Replace with a suitable needle (see pages 14–15) and see if the stitch appearance improves. Old blunt needles may be to blame. Skipped stitches may also be due to thread that is too tight and not sliding through the guides smoothly. Check and re-thread if necessary. Finally, if the problem remains, check how the needle is inserted and threaded. The flat part of the shaft goes to the back with the rounded end and groove at the front when in place. The thread should lie in the groove.
Note: Most modern machine needles are threaded from front to back while some older models are threaded from left to right.

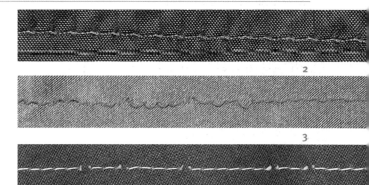

2 Stitch holes appear with stitches: Change the needle to a finer one that will not make such large holes. Use fine needles with fine fabrics.

3 Loose stitches: The stitch length is too long for the fabric being sewn. Decrease the length slightly and try again.

4 Breaking stitches: These are often caused by using a straight stitch on a stretchy fabric – when the fabric is stretched, the thread snaps. Use polyester-covered cotton thread for greater stretchability, and sew seams with small zigzag stitches.

Material matters

Today's modern fabrics are constructed from natural and synthetic fibres, sometimes even mixed or blended together. They are often finished with processes which improve their hand, colour-fastness and laundering properties. This gives a great range of choice, but also requires more knowledge to get the best results from each length of cloth you buy. As well as giving factual information about different types of material, this chapter offers advice on sewing, handling and storing fabrics.

Fibre facts

Natural fibres are the fine individual filaments or strands that are spun and twisted with others to form yarns and fabrics, and include cotton, wool, linen, hemp and silk. Man-made and synthetic fibres include viscose rayon, acetate, acrylic, nylon, polyester, microfibre and spandex. The type of fibre will affect the handling of a fabric, so it is important to know what it is – read on to find out more.

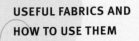

Ten
USEFUL FABRICS AND HOW TO USE THEM

There are many fabrics available in a huge range of weights and textures, with different fibre contents in all sorts of colours and patterns. Here are ten of the most useful types of fabric, great for today's styles of clothing, household items and soft furnishings.

Silk fibre comes from the silk moth at the stage of its development when it is a caterpillar and spins itself a cocoon. The cocoon is formed by the raw silk fibre which is unravelled and spun to form silk threads which are then woven into fabric.

Linen comes from the pretty blue-flowered flax plant. The fibres are sourced from the stem and are then spun and woven to form linen fabrics.

Denim, although originally work-wear fabric, is popular for everyday styles today.

Wool fibre from sheep and other animals makes a range of yarn and fabrics we recognize as woollen cloth. These may be fine like worsted cloth, coloured weaves like tartan, or chunky and knitted into sweaters.

The soft, relatively short fibres of cotton are found in the cotton boll of the cotton plant, a shrub which grows in warm countries. It is a popular fibre producing various woven and knitted fabrics.

	1 DENIM	2 COTTON KNIT	3 FLEECE FABRIC	4 MUSLIN
PROPERTIES	This strong, hard wearing, absorbent woven fabric is made from cotton. It has been transformed from workwear to fashion and is a popular cloth for everyday garments.	Knitted cotton – the type used for T-shirts – is a very versatile fabric as its stretch makes it comfortable to wear and easy to fit. It can be plain, dyed or printed, and is absorbent and comfortable next to the skin. Complex seams and darts are unnecessary and fastenings aren't usually required.	Synthetic fleece has a slight stretch, which makes it comfortable and easy to wear. It is soft, warm and lightweight. Fleece can be treated to prevent 'pilling' and can be made into simple-shaped garments, often not requiring fastenings or detailed seam shaping.	This stable, closely woven, natural-coloured fabric is seldom used for fashion but is vital for toile (pretest) garments. It comes in various weights, is easy to handle and sew, and its stable nature makes it ideal for testing prototype designs.
SUITABLE FOR	Jeans, jackets, shirts, slipcovers and children's wear.	T-shirts, stretch tops and dresses, and underwear.	Sweaters, jackets and cold-weather wear.	Toile (pretest) garments, bags and carriers, and under covers beneath slipcovers.
TIPS	• If the denim is too tough for pins, use weights instead. • Cut with long-bladed scissors. Use a jeans needle (size 14 or 16) and sew with flat fell or mock flat fell seams (see pages 81–82). • Construct with strong thread and use orange or gold topstitching thread to add an authentic 'denim style'.	• Cover the work surface with a cotton sheet before spreading out the cotton knit for cutting. This prevents it from slipping or stretching. • Cut with shears or a rotary cutter on a self-healing mat. • Sew seams with a serger or use a walking foot (see page 24) on a sewing machine. • Choose a ballpoint or stretch needle and sew with a stretch stitch or narrow zigzag.	• Use weights or very long pins and cut with shears. Cut all fabric pieces in the same direction, as the fabric has a nap. • Sew seams with a serger or attach a walking foot to the sewing machine and stitch with a stretch stitch or narrow zigzag. Lengthen the stitch to 8spi (3mm) and use a size 11–14 needle.	• Cut with long-bladed scissors and sew with a size 11–14 needle (depending on cloth weight). • Choose plain or flat fell seams and neaten raw edges with a serger, zigzag stitch or pinking shears.

Modern faux suede is much easier to cut, sew and launder than natural suede skin.

	5 SILK DUPIONI	6 TOWELLING	7 FAUX SUEDE
PROPERTIES	This silk fabric has a slight sheen and an interesting slub texture caused by the natural, uneven threads in the weave. It is medium weight with a crisp finish. Incredibly easy to work with and behaving a bit like paper, it handles and sews easily and can be controlled with the heat of the iron.	Towels are made from cotton because of their ability to absorb water. The surface loops on both sides of the cloth increase the surface area, further improving its absorption properties.	Artificial suede-like fabrics have become increasingly realistic in recent years. Either woven or knitted, and generally made from microfibre, they have a brushed surface to give the appearance of suede. They are easy to care for and launder, and available in a convenient roll.
SUITABLE FOR	Jackets and evening or bridal wear, as well as lampshades, curtains, and cushions.	Towels, robes and beachwear.	Skirts, coats, jackets and soft furnishings.
TIPS	• Cut with shears and, if necessary, neaten raw edges before sewing seams as they may fray. • Sew with a size 11 needle and choose plain seams. • Use the iron as a tool to press flat edges before stitching them.	• Use weights or long pins to secure pattern pieces and cut with shears. • Keep a vacuum cleaner handy to control the tiny pieces of pile that are released during cutting. • Sew with a size 11 or 14 needle and increase the stitch length to 8spi (3mm). Sew with a good quality cotton thread.	• Weights are better than pins when attaching pattern pieces for cutting out. • Sew with a microtex needle and choose a stitch length of 8–10spi (2.5–3mm). • Mock flat fell seams and simple top stitched hems work well. Use a walking foot for best results.

8 100% SILK ORGANZA	9 SPANDEX	10 SHEETING
This fine, sheer silk is very strong as a result of its highly spun threads. It is stable but lightweight and thin, and withstands the heat of a hot iron.	Spandex has great stretch and recovery properties. It is blended with other fibres to achieve particular qualities in a fabric. Spandex is added to suiting to retain the shape of jackets (elbows) and trousers (knees), and its stretch and comfort make it ideal for sportswear.	A plain weave cotton or cotton mix fabric that is available in widths up to 2.65m (106in), sheeting is often plain dyed but can also be printed. The extra width makes it useful for various applications where seams joining narrower widths would be undesirable, such as bedding. When polyester is mixed with the cotton fibre, the laundering properties are improved, allowing faster drying.
Evening wear, underlining to stabilize other fabrics, pressing cloths and curtains.	Sportswear, dancewear, lingerie, tailored jackets, trousers and skirts.	Sheets, pillowcases and duvet covers.
• Use sharp shears and hold paper patterns in place with long pins, or cut with a rotary cutter and mat. • Sew with a size 9 or 11 needle and a stitch length of 10spi (2.5mm). • Choose delicate French or hairline seams (since the fabric is sheer) and rolled hems sewn on a sewing machine or serger.	• Use long, sharp pins or weights and sharp shears to cut. • Sew with a ballpoint or stretch needle and select a stretch stitch or narrow zigzag. • A walking foot attachment will prevent the fabric stretching during sewing, or use a serger to construct seams.	• Easy to cut and sew with no special advice required.

Silk fabrics have a beautiful light-reflecting quality, making them comfortable to wear and lovely to look at.

39 Fabric facts

Fibres, from one or more sources, are generally spun together to form yarns, which are then woven or knitted into fabric. Occasionally the fibres are bonded directly together to form a felted fabric. Fabrics are constructed in three main ways.

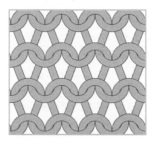

Woven

A stable fabric with yarns woven together at 90 degrees that stretches only when pulled diagonally across the grain. Examples include cotton or polyester sheeting, woollen tweed, table linen and acetate lining.

Knitted

The loop formation makes for a stretchy fabric, such as woollen knitwear, cotton T-shirting and sweatshirting.

Non-woven

This does not stretch and is fairly stable but it does not have the strength of a woven fabric. Examples include craft felt, disposable nappies, interfacing and batting.

FIX IT

40 Lost the label?

If you want to know what a fabric is made from, a burn test will help you identify the fibre. Using tongs to hold the fabric over a fireproof mat, light a small swatch of fabric with a taper or match and observe how it burns. Keep a bucket of water close by as a precaution.

Cotton and linen (from vegetable fibres)
Both cotton and linen catch fire easily and burn well (like paper) but are easily extinguished. The remaining ash crumbles easily.

Wool and silk (protein fibres)
Wool does not light easily and when the fire source is removed it will often go out. Silk catches light more easily. Both give off a smell similar to burning hair and leave a crumbling ash.

Acetate and viscose rayon (from cellulose)
Acetate burns well, the flame is difficult to blow out and the ash that remains is hard. Viscose rayon also burns well, but it gives off a woody smell and leaves only a small amount of ash.

Nylon, acrylic and polyester (derived from coal/oil/petroleum)
These fibres burn easily and leave a black bead of residue or hard ash when cooled. Nylon smells of burning plastic, while polyester has a sweeter smell. Fabrics made from a mixture of fibres will be more difficult to identify.

A burn test helps to identify the fibre a fabric is made from. Watch how it reacts to a flame, how it burns and the appearance of the residue. Always take care when working with a lit match.

Choosing fabrics

Most people who sew are fascinated by fabric and buy lots of it. Often they fall for the colour or design and 'have to have it', only for the length of carefully chosen cloth to lie untouched for months or years. The joy of handling the fabric and anticipating what it will be made into provides as much pleasure as actually sewing it into a garment.

Where do I start?

You may browse a fabric shop with a specific design in mind, or it may be the case that a specific fabric just jumps out at you. Whatever the case, follow your instincts.

Design first

It may be a dress for a special occasion, a request from a child for a particular soft toy, or a T-shirt for a summer holiday, but the idea or design emerges first. The next task is to find a suitable fabric for the project. This may take some time since local fabric shops may not stock what you have in mind.

If you have chosen a commercial pattern, consult the packet to find how much fabric is required; if you are working from a photograph or sketch, browse through commercial patterns to find similar designs. Write the information in a small notebook and carry it with you everywhere until you find the right fabric.

Fabric first

You spot a beautiful lace, silk or colourful printed fabric in a shop and simply must buy it. It may take some time to visualize the most appropriate design for it and to find the perfect paper pattern to sew it up. In this case, it is important to buy sufficient material at the outset to avoid disappointment later.

When buying fabric from a shop, ask for details of the fibre content and care requirements. Label each fabric in your stash with these details for future reference.

To prevent cut edges fraying while in storage, overlock or zigzag stitch them before you put the fabric away. Fabrics liable to shrinkage may also be laundered before storage, so they will be ready to use whenever you want them.

Important considerations

There are many questions you should ask yourself if you wish to be more practical about selecting fabric. No doubt you will continue to make spontaneous purchases from time to time, but it is useful to bear the following points in mind.

Purpose

How will the garment or project be worn or used? Sportswear needs to be comfortable and stretchy, so choose knitted cotton with spandex. A toddler's dress must be comfortable yet hard wearing and easily laundered, so a bright, colourfast cotton print would be suitable.

Colour

Choose colours to suit the wearer's colouring and personality as well as the occasion. Bright red satin is ideal for a party dress but less appropriate for a skirt worn to the office.

Texture

Consider the texture of the cloth in conjunction with the design and the purpose. Velvet has a thick, dense pile while satin has a smooth, shiny surface. Either of these are great for seldom-worn, special-occasion wear but not for everyday children's clothing or for work, as the appearance deteriorates rapidly with frequent washing and wearing.

Weight

The chosen design may require a sheer, transparent fabric or a heavier cloth. Consider the options carefully before buying the one that is most suitable for the look required.

Hand

Feel the fabric to determine its hand. Some fabrics drape delicately (slinky knit) while others are crisp and firm (taffeta). Some crease easily (cotton, linen) yet others are bouncy and resist creasing (polyester, crêpe de Chine). A soft draping cloth will not hold pleats and a crisp fabric will not work as a cowl neckline – so choose a suitable fabric for the design.

Wardrobe

Consider your existing garments and how new fabrics and garments will fit into the scheme. Do you really need a sixth pink frilly skirt or will a bright emerald blouse match the pastel skirts and trousers you already own?

Season

Select mostly mid-weight fabrics for garments that can be worn for most of the year. A thick black bouclé coat may be beautiful but only wearable for a month in deepest winter, while a medium-weight woollen jacket will give more practical use from autumn through winter to spring.

Working with tricky fabrics

When learning to sew, choose stable, natural fabrics as these are easy to handle. Having mastered the basics, move on to more difficult fabrics. Always test out a new fabric before starting a project to avoid disappointment.

43

Eight
SOLUTIONS FOR TRICKY TEXTILES

1 Stretch

Cotton knit, sweatshirt fabric, slinky knit, fabrics containing spandex.

Solutions: Use a serger or attach a walking foot to the sewing machine and select a preprogrammed stretch stitch or a narrow zigzag.

2 Fraying edges

Satin, loosely woven wools, some woven linens, viscose rayons.

Solutions: Neaten raw edges immediately after cutting and before sewing the seams with a serger or zigzag machine stitch. Alternatively, cut out with pinking shears.

3 Heat sensitive

Nylon, polyester, acrylic, acetate, microfibre, wool.

Solutions: Use a pressing cloth to protect the fabric, or reduce the heat and the pressure applied to the fabric.

4 Harsh and hard

Waterproof coated fabrics, faux leather, blackout lining, upholstery fabrics and canvas.

Solutions: Use weights or masking tape in place of pins and select a strong needle (size 14 or 16). Consider a leather needle for some projects.

5 Loose weave

Silk and wool tweed-type fabrics.

Solutions: Underline with silk organza or a fine fusible interfacing to stabilize the fabric and lengthen the life of the garment. Consider neatening edges before construction.

6 Sheers

Chiffon, voile, organza, lace.

Solutions: Select a new fine needle (size 9) and shorten the stitch length. Join with narrow French or hairline seams to give a delicate finish.

7 Thick and dense

Fleece, boiled wool, upholstery fabric, chenille, wool and silk tweeds.

Solutions: Fit a walking foot attachment and lengthen the stitch to 7–8spi (3–3.5mm). Use a strong needle in a size 14 or 16.

8 Slippery

Fine satins and silks, slinky knits.

Solutions: Cover the work surface with a cotton sheet before laying out the fabric in a single layer for cutting out. The short cotton fibres 'grip' the slippery fabric and keep it stable while cutting.

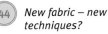

Storing fabrics

Having purchased fabric, it is important to look after it properly until it is made up into the perfect garment, toy, pillow or quilt. Consider storage carefully to avoid damage from creasing, light, odours and pests.

45 Avoid creases

If fabric has been folded and put in a bag, creases may become permanently set. If this is the case, remove the fabric and roll it onto a tube with the right side in, to keep it flat. Place the roll of fabric in a bag to keep it clean. The back of a cupboard may provide a suitable home for the roll until there is time to make up the fabric. Alternatively, refold carefully and peg a length of fabric to a coat hanger and hang in the wardrobe.

46 Use pest deterrents

Pests, such as moths and beetles, may eat away at fabric stashes. The best way to keep on top of this problem is to vacuum fabric storage chests and cupboards regularly. Lavender bags do not really keep moths at bay, although they smell nice.

47 Maintain odour-free fabric

Fabrics have a tendency to pick up odours, such as cigarette smoke and cooking smells. In open-plan homes without doors it is important to keep fabric in plastic boxes with well-fitting lids or in sealed bags – and as far away from the kitchen as possible.

48 Be wary of light sources

Folded piles of fabric may look lovely on open shelves, but this may not be the best way to store them long-term. Although open shelves make selecting colours and prints easy, if the room is very bright, light may affect the fabric. Consider protecting fabrics from the light with a cloth curtain or buying a traditional cupboard with doors.

49 Keep your fabric dry

Do not store fabric when damp. If fabric is washed or steam pressed to preshrink it, make sure it is completely dry before storing it.

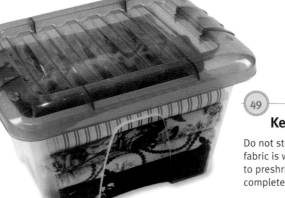

FIX IT

50 How should I store projects during construction?

Always fold curtains lengthwise and never across the width. Any stubborn creases left in the length will be lost in the folds when the curtains are hung, but creases across the fabric may not easily fall out. Fold lengthwise with the right side of the fabric on the inside. If possible, leave flat on a spare bed. If this is not possible, fold in three, placing cardboard tubes under the folds for support. Keep the full skirts of wedding gowns and evening wear flat and loosely wrapped in a large clean sheet.

Working with colour

There are many things to think about when choosing fabric to suit the wearer, the occasion or purpose. Colour, pattern or print, and texture are particularly important.

Getting to grips with the colour wheel

Colour choice is important when choosing fabrics for garment making. For example, a young woman with dark hair may look fantastic in a scarlet jacket unless she is shy and feels that the brightness of the red draws unnecessary attention to her. However, in a black jacket, which she may feel safer in, she might appear tired and pale, as the darkness of the black will draw any colour from her face. A brown or navy with splashes of colour in smaller areas would be a good choice.

Whether you have a good eye for colour, or need advice from an expert, find out what colours work for you and flatter your own colouring. The colour wheel (right) is a good place to start. Colours diametrically opposite each other on the wheel, like orange and blue, are known as 'complementary colours' and create bold contrasts when used side by side in a single garment or outfit. Colours next to each other on the wheel (red, orange-red, orange, yellow-orange, yellow, for example) could be described as being part of an analogous colour range or scheme. These are known as 'harmonious colours' and usually sit well together.

How to choose colour for rooms and furnishings

The same rules apply for choosing colours to decorate rooms as they do for garments. When choosing fabrics, furniture or paint, go for the mood you require and the shades and tones of colour you want to live with. Choose blue for a cool effect in bedrooms and bathrooms, or yellow and orange for a bright and cheerful kitchen. Why not paint and furnish a room around a single item, such as these pink and green cushions (below).

Use the colour wheel to help get your colour balance right.

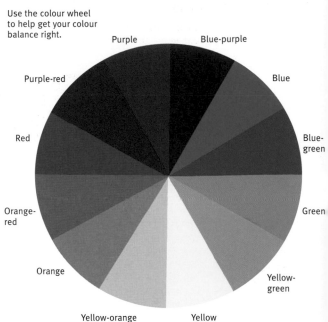

Purple · Blue-purple · Blue · Blue-green · Green · Yellow-green · Yellow · Yellow-orange · Orange · Orange-red · Red · Purple-red

54

What do colours say?

Although colour is a subjective experience, most colours portray a mood and convey a statement to others.

- **White:** Clean and fresh
Used for medical uniforms, traditional wedding dresses in some cultures, newborn baby clothes and christening outfits, white is a pure colour.

- **Black:** Sophisticated
Some people choose black because they do not wish to stand out in a crowd, while others will wear this simple, elegant colour to look sophisticated.

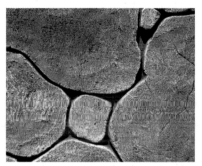

- **Grey:** Efficient and businesslike
Light and dark greys are often chosen for suits and clothes for the office and can imply practicality and efficiency.

- **Brown:** Relaxed
Shades of brown, from dark to light beige, are neutral but can, like black, give the impression of safety. Brown is less threatening than black and has a more easy-going feel.

- **Blue**. Cool and trustworthy
Whether navy, washed denim or baby blue, there is a shade to suit everyone.

- **Red**: Confident
Red gives off an energy that implies the wearer is confident and determined.

- **Yellow:** Cheerful
Yellow says spring, hope, optimism and freshness. It makes the wearer and those around him or her more cheerful.

- **Green:** Calm and reassuring
Green is the colour of grass, trees and the countryside, creating a calming influence.

- **Pink and lilac:** Sensitive and creative
When white and/or blue are added to red it loses its intensity and gives softer shades, implying the wearer is sensitive.

Pattern and printed fabrics

While colour is crucial in selecting fabric for clothes and home furnishings, pattern – whether woven in or printed – makes even more of a statement about you. Floral prints are feminine, spots and dots can be fun, and geometric patterns are regular and logical.

 55
Fashion influences

Patterns, even more so than colour and figure silhouette, are affected by fast-changing fashions. A particular style of design popular one season may be dropped the next. Buy fashionable prints for one-off garments worn for a special occasion and choose more traditional patterned fabric for clothes that will have a longer life.

58
Choosing pattern for furnishing

Choose patterns – floral, geometric, traditional or contemporary – to suit the rooms and also the occupant's age and personality. It is important to consider the size and proportions of the room, the function of the room and how frequently it will be redecorated.

60
Bright and bold

Just as bright primary colours can draw attention to the wearer, so can large, bold prints. If this suits your personality then be brave and bold, but if you wish to make less of a statement about yourself choose a smaller, more neutral design. Bold prints also add pounds to a figure, so if you wish to conceal your shape or size select a more modest design. Or choose a bold pattern for a part of your figure that you like and want to show off.

 56
Balancing colour and print

Choose a patterned fabric you love and pick up one or two plain colours to complete the look. An all-over pattern in a bright, large print may be too much for a dress but would look good made into a shirt and worn with plain, coordinating trousers. When accessorizing, steer clear of picking too many of the colours from the pattern as this may give a haphazard effect, but don't go mad with one colour, choosing matching shoes, purse, jewellery, hat, gloves, scarf...

 59
Choosing for patchwork

Patchwork is a technique that mixes different colours and prints together in creative ways. Fabrics for patchwork are best if colourfast, 100 per cent cotton and all the same weight. Consider the use of the quilt or project and select colours and prints accordingly – pastels for babies and perhaps novelty prints for children that work in harmony with each other. Small prints are successful for small templates and larger prints for bigger areas.

 **61**
Small prints

A small print on a fabric may be perfect for a patchwork project but look pale and insipid when made into a dress or skirt. Choose small patterns carefully or mix them with plain colours.

57
Check out the selvedge!

Printed fabrics usually have a series of dots along the selvedge indicating the individual colours used in the screen printing process. Use these colour dots to coordinate or group your other fabrics. Make sure you use the less dominant colours in the selvedge too, to liven up your project.

MAKE IT!

A nine-square cushion

A simple project for a new patchwork student is to make a cushion from nine 15cm (6in) squares. It gives the opportunity to choose two printed fabrics that work well together and encourages accurate cutting, sewing and matching.

1 Choose two fabric prints and cut nine 15cm (6in) squares – five in one colour and four in the other.

2 Arrange and pin together in strips of three and then sew together with 6mm (¼in) seams.

3 Pin and sew the strips together carefully, matching the joins of the squares, and press the seam allowances to one side.

4 Cut two rectangles measuring 22 x 43cm (17 x 9in) for the back of the cushion. Sew a 41cm (16in) zip into the seam to join the two rectangles and form a square.

5 Open the zip and place the front and back cushion pieces together with right sides facing. Pin and sew around the outside and neaten raw edges.

6 Turn through and fill with a cushion pad.

Texture and weight

The feel of cloth is vital for comfort and style when making clothes. Choose fabric for a project on the basis of its weight, thickness, crispness, softness and transparency. Each sewing task requires a specific fabric quality.

63 Know your project

The fabric used to make swimwear is very different from the fabric used to make curtains. Make sure you have the correct fabric or your project could go very wrong.

Curtains

Curtains can be thick for warmth and to keep the light out, or sheer for a delicate window dressing to decorate the window or to give some privacy. Suggested fabrics include:

• Velvet
• Velveteen
• Faux suede
• Voile

Raincoat

Strong and waterproof to fulfil their function, raincoats are light and water-repellent. Suggested fabrics include:

• Vinyl
• Ripstop nylon
• Coated cotton poplin
• Microfibre

Swimwear

Strong, lightweight, non-absorbent and stretchy for figure-hugging comfort and easy movement. Suggested fabrics include:

• Polyester/elastane mix
• Nylon/elastane mix

Grecian-style evening dress

Soft draping fabric that falls in gentle folds creating fluid 3-D lines. Suggested fabrics include:

• Slinky knit
• Crêpe de Chine
• Chiffon
• Habutai silk
• Liquid satin

Tailored skirt

Strong fabric with weight to ensure it holds its shape and does not seat with wear. Suggested fabrics include:

• Tartan
• Worsted wool
• Velvet
• Silk tweed

Tablecloth

Smooth, crease-free and easy to wash, with enough weight to drape well over the edges. Suggested fabrics include:

• 100 per cent cotton
• Linen
• Polyester
• Microfibre

64 Wash it!

Fabric quality can change after washing – it can shrink, soften or crinkle. If you prewash the fabric you will know what you're working with from the start. Garments, curtains or soft furnishings that will be dry-cleaned do not need to be prewashed before cutting out and making up.

Take care to select appropriate fabric for each project you sew.

65

What is 'nap', and how do I test for it?

Commercial patterns often include special cutting layouts for 'with nap' fabrics – that is, fabrics with a directional texture or pattern.

Fabrics 'with nap' include pile fabrics (such as velvet, chenille and faux fur) and brushed fabrics, such as brushed denim. Run your hand over the fabric; it will feel smooth in one direction and rough in the other, because the fuzzy surface lies slightly flatter in one lengthwise direction (up or down the length). For an even appearance, all pattern pieces should be cut out with the pile running in the same direction. For better wear, cut out such fabrics with the nap running downwards.

Some smooth fabrics are also directional, such as shot silks, satins, and iridescent fabrics. If the pieces are not cut in the same direction, the colour effect will vary from one piece to another.

To test such fabrics for nap, fold the fabric across the width, with right sides together, then fold one corner of the top layer across, as shown. If the two exposed right side surfaces differ in appearance, treat the fabric as 'with nap'. Patterned fabrics that are one-directional should also be treated as 'with nap' fabrics.

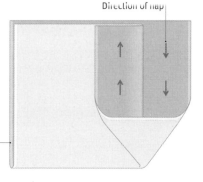

Direction of nap

Selvedges

Check if fabric has a nap or direction before cutting out.

66

Sewing with pile or 'with nap' fabrics

1 Cut pieces on a single layer of fabric, flipping the pattern over to get left and right sides. Stitch in the direction of the pile or nap.

2 Trim fur pile from the seam allowance to reduce bulk.

3 Use a pin to pick out pile trapped in the seam stitching.

68

Pressing with pile or 'with nap' fabrics

When pressing pile fabrics, use a needleboard, soft terry towel or layer of self-fabric. Always press lightly from the reverse using a press cloth.

Take care when ironing napped fabrics.

TRY IT

67 *What's a feel test?*

It is important to handle fabric before buying it. Your eyes can only give you part of the information; feeling a piece of cloth can tell you so much more about its quality and properties. Knowledge about fabrics is gained over many years – and handling the cloth is an essential part of the learning process.

1 Stroke the surface to check if it has a pile or is harsh or smooth to the touch.

2 Hold it in your hand and crunch to see whether it creases or instantly straightens out.

3 Grab and pull the fabric to see whether it stretches and, if it does, whether it returns to its natural state slowly or instantly.

Sourcing fabrics

It can be difficult to find the perfect material and accessories for a project at local fabric shops but there are other options, like the Internet, that have opened up many more possibilities in recent years.

69

Fabric options

From the web to your local charity shop, fabric suppliers come in diverse outfits.

Fabric shops

Purchasing fabric from a store is probably the most fulfilling way to source cloth but a diminishing interest in home sewing in some parts of the world means that many traditional fabric shops have closed down or reduced their range. It is therefore more difficult for some people to get access to good supplies of fabric and notions.

Mail order

Although it is not as pleasing or practical to buy fabric by mail order – nothing compares with viewing and handling full lengths of cloth on the bale or roll – most companies will send samples and swatches to view at home. They may respond to an individual's request to send a number of swatches for a particular project or, for a small fee, they may send out seasonal ranges to customers two or three times a year. Although it is convenient to select fabrics at home, it can be difficult visualizing the entire effect of a pattern from a small swatch.

Online auction sites

A fun way to buy fabric, notions, and sewing tools is through an online auction site such as eBay. Real bargains may be had this way, although there may be disappointment if the items do not turn out exactly as anticipated when they arrive.

Sewing magazines

Classified and personal ads in sewing, craft or patchwork magazines may offer the chance to source fabrics. Subscribe to your favourite magazine to ensure it arrives early and gives you a better chance of obtaining the fabrics offered in these ads.

Flea markets

Flea markets often source their fabrics from factories, buying up ends of rolls from clothing manufacturers. This offers the chance to buy unusual fabrics or, sometimes, designer fabrics not available from fabric shops. Quantities will, however, be limited and will not be available on a long-term basis – once it has been sold there will not be any more.

Clothing factories

If a clothing manufacturer has an outlet that sells its wares direct from the factory, it may offer short lengths of fabric that are left after making up its ranges. Although limited, such a fabric may provide what is needed.

Swapping

Sewing or craft groups that meet on a regular basis sometimes hold swap meetings for fabric, patterns, threads, etc. It gives people the opportunity to reduce their own stashes and replenish with new designs for fresh inspiration. Why not suggest this to your group?

Charity shops

Be creative when looking for fabric for a project. Consider buying garments from a charity shop to cut down to size. For example, leather skirts make perfect purses, and curtains or bedding are ideal for shopping bags. Knitwear, especially large men's sweaters, can be cut down to make children's sweaters or hats.

MAKE IT!

70

What can I do with mail-order swatches?

Use the tiny mail-order samples to make a purse.

1 Cut a piece of muslin about 30cm (12in) square as a backing fabric. Select swatches of all textures in colours that work together.

2 Arrange the swatches over the backing. Use temporary spray adhesive to hold them in place.

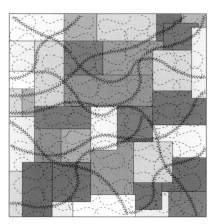

3 Thread the sewing machine with a metallic floss or thread and sew the swatches to the backing with haphazard lines of stitching.

4 Trim the edges of the newly-created fabric and cut a piece of lining in the same size. Fold the new fabric in half, top edges together with the right sides facing. Sew the sides together with a 1.5cm (⅝in) seam, then turn through to the right side. Make up the lining in the same way.

5 Tuck down the top edges of the purse and lining. Slip the lining inside the bag (with wrong sides facing) and pin the layers together along the top. Take out some of the pins and ease the handles in between the lining and bag, then replace the pins to hold the horizontal part of the handle in place. Secure with small slip stitches removing the pins in the process.

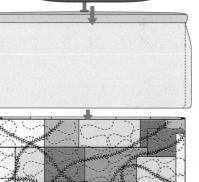

Special products

New products may emerge and older ones may be developed with new uses in mind. Make use of the following toolkit essentials to speed up the sewing process, simplify methods or improve the finish.

Stabilizing films

Stabilizers are required for good results in machine embroidery (see page 68). A clear film of stabilizer, which washes away or disappears when heat is applied, is particularly useful in some circumstances. It works well when placed over the surface of towelling (so that embroidery doesn't sink into the pile) and for making lace.

Adhesive tapes and fusible webs

These products melt with the heat of an iron and turn to glue, sticking the adjacent materials together. They are available in strips of varying widths and larger pieces on a roll. The thinnest strips are used to temporarily hold tapes and ribbons in position before being sewn permanently in place. Wider strips are used to shorten hems on trousers and larger sheets are used for appliqué projects (see pages 138–140). They have a paper backing to make them easier to handle.

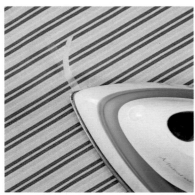

1 Iron the fusible strip into place with the glue side down.

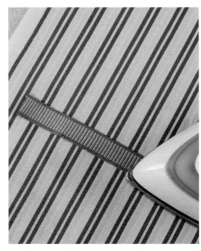

3 Place the ribbon over the glue strip and iron in position.

Fusible interfacings

The latest generation of fusible interfacings are constructed so that they move sufficiently to work with the fabrics they are fixed to. They are soft and add the necessary depth and weight to areas of a garment and remain unseen from the outside.

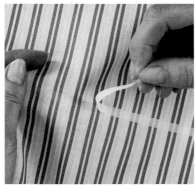

2 Peel away the paper covering.

Clear elastic

A clear elastic is now available that is ideal for swimwear as it does not deteriorate with chlorine from swimming pools. It is also useful for stabilizing shoulders and is sewn into the seam to prevent stretching.

TRY IT

 75 *Secret underlinings*

The construction of a garment or project on the inside often goes unnoticed but gives the finished outer look its essential qualities. A fine, delicate silk fabric can be used for a firm, straight skirt or a structured bodice – but only if support is provided beneath it. The qualities of any fabric can be altered by carefully chosen underlinings.

When worn, the canvas underlining holds the shape of the bodice, giving a smooth, flat appearance.

Collar and cuff canvas

This stiff interlining is intended to support the cuffs and collars of men's shirts. It is also perfect for corset-type bodices to support softer fabrics.

1 Cut out the pattern pieces in fabric, cotton lawn, and collar and cuff canvas. Trim away the seam allowances from the canvas and mount it onto the centre of the cotton lawn with quilting stitches.

2 Place the cotton lawn and canvas onto the fabric and stitch around the outside to join the layers together. Make up the garment by sewing the prepared panels together, stitching through the softer layers.

Stiff net

Stiff net is used to support fabric for a skirt when a full silhouette is required. A soft draping silk, for example, will not have the crispness to support itself when making a full gathered skirt.

To provide support, place a layer of stiff dress net beneath the silk and make up as one. If the honeycomb pattern of the net shows through, place a layer of cotton lawn between the silk and the net. Be creative and work various layers together to give the required look.

Alternatively, use many layers of tulle as a feature to hold the shape of the skirt rather than a more subtle underlining.

Batting and fleece

This is generally used for quilting but is perfect for personalized shoulder pads. A jacket or coat should not rely on the body for support and must have an internal hanger to show the garment at its best.

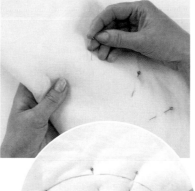
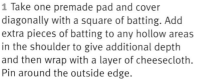

1 Take one premade pad and cover diagonally with a square of batting. Add extra pieces of batting to any hollow areas in the shoulder to give additional depth and then wrap with a layer of cheesecloth. Pin around the outside edge.

2 Quilt with a long straight stitch, starting from the front edge, working around the outside of the pad, and spiralling towards the centre. Manipulate the pad into a saddle or shoulder shape and trim to the size required. Neaten the outside edge and sew in place.

Threads and more threads

There are many types of thread on the market for all kinds of sewing. Strong, functional threads are necessary for constructing garments and soft furnishings, while decorative threads with more sheen or texture can be bought for embroidery and embellishment.

77

Four

RULES FOR PICKING THE RIGHT THREAD

TRY IT

76 *Can't thread your needle?*

Threading needles can be very frustrating. Try these suggestions to speed up the process.

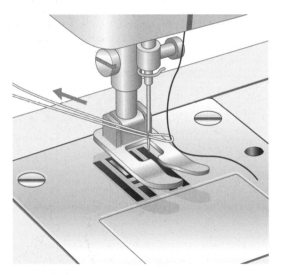

Use a folded carrier thread to pull through a stubborn thread.

- Cut the thread end at an angle.

- Lick the thread end if using cotton. This does not work with polyester thread, as it is not absorbent.

- Lick the needle not the thread! Some people swear by this trick and say it always works. But be careful!

- For fluffy or decorative threads use a 'carrier'. This is a length of fine thread folded in half into which the decorative thread is placed (turn to page 72 for more details).

- Use a needle threader. These vary in design from a flattened circle or small diamond of wire with a metal handle to more complex little gadgets (see page 12).

1 Match the fibre

Choose good quality thread in a fibre similar to the fabric being sewn: cotton thread for cotton and linen fabric; polyester for synthetic fabrics; silk for silk and woollen cloth. If a cotton dress has been sewn up with polyester thread, for example, the thread may melt in the washing machine if the setting is too hot.

2 Good quality

Choose good quality thread. There is nothing more disappointing than when cheap thread disintegrates and a garment falls apart. This is especially important for raincoats, as some threads can be weakened by water. Better threads have a smoother twist with an even thickness. These give better results and are less damaging to sewing machines.

3 Colour

Finding a perfect colour match for thread and fabric can be difficult. Choose a slightly darker shade of thread, as it will be hidden in the shade of a seam, rather than a lighter shade, which may be more noticeable.

4 Basting

Thread used for basting should not be as strong as general sewing thread. As a temporary thread, it must not damage fabric when it is removed. Choose a contrasting colour.

(78) Functional threads

Read on to ensure you choose the correct thread for your project.

General-purpose threads

These may be spun from polyester or mercerized cotton or have a cotton core covered with polyester. Use them on your sewing machine or serger for making garments or soft furnishing projects.

Silk threads

Silk thread is easier to handle and is less likely to tangle or become knotted.

Woolly nylons

Normally available on large cones, these are perfect for the loopers when serger sewing. The loosely spun finish spreads over the edge for a softer effect.

Bobbin fill

This extra-fine smooth thread is used in the bobbin when doing machine embroidery. A greater length can be fitted onto a spool and it reduces the bulk of an embroidered design. As it is very fine, only the embroidery floss is seen on the surface. It is also more economical as it uses less embroidery thread.

TRY IT

 (79) *Is there any use for thread ends?*

Collect the thread ends from all your sewing tasks instead of throwing them away. When you have gathered a sufficient quantity, cut a piece of muslin and spread the thread pieces over the backing cloth. Cover with a layer of stabilizer film, which will eventually be washed away, and baste in place. With a decorative thread on the sewing machine, sew rows of stitching through all layers until there is enough stitching to hold the threads in place. Wash in warm water to remove the film, then dry. Use the piece to make a small purse or a glasses case.

With a decorative machine stitch, sew over the loose coloured threads to hold them in place and create an interesting new fabric.

FIX IT

80 *At a loose end?*

Working with thread can be a frustrating process. Read on to learn a few tips and techniques that may make your life that little bit easier.

Separating stranded floss

Cut the threads flat and tap the end to spread them apart. This makes it easier to select the number of strands to grab and pull out.

Topstitch thread alternatives

If you cannot find topstitch thread in the required colour, wind some general-purpose thread onto a bobbin and sew using both the spool and bobbin through the needle to give a stronger effect. Alternatively, use the triple stitch normally used for stretch fabric. The effect of the thread sewing back and forwards makes a thicker line of topstitching.

Short lengths

Cut short lengths of thread when hand sewing. Longer lengths knot more readily and slow the sewing process down.

Cutting direction

When taking thread from a spool, do not thread the cut end through the eye. The thread has a direction and is intended to be sewn from the wound end first.

Springy thread

Some decorative threads are harsh and springy and slip off the spool, getting caught underneath. An old pair of tights can be cut into small lengths and placed over the spool to hold the threads in place and prevent the threads from slipping off.

81 Decorative threads

If you are looking to embellish your project, there are various decorative threads on the market to choose from.

Machine embroidery floss

This is available in a huge range of colours made from rayon, polyester, cotton and even wool. Some flosses have a high sheen while others have duller surface textures for a variety of effects.

Metallic threads

These vary from a fine flat filament to a solid core covered with metallic threads. Use them for hand sewing and on the sewing machine but choose a metallic needle, which has a larger eye and does not shred the thread.

Topstitch thread

This is stronger, thicker thread that gives a bolder finish. Use it for topstitching and edge stitching seams, hand sewing buttonholes and for sewing on buttons securely.

82 Hand embroidery threads

There are many different types of embroidery threads available, each with their own characteristics. The beginner will find cotton floss and pearl cotton no. 5 the easiest to work with, but other, more unusual threads such as silks and metallics will add their own special touch to your work.

Cotton floss

Cotton floss is supplied in small skeins, with six strands loosely wound together. Strands may be separated and combined to make up any weight of thread required, making it suitable for any size project. Cotton floss is widely available in a huge range of colours, both plain and shade-dyed.

Soft embroidery cotton

A soft, rounded, heavy thread with a matt finish, which may not be separated into finer strands. Use this thread for bold stitching on large projects in heavy weight fabrics.

Silk floss

Silk floss is similar in weight to cotton floss and used in the same way. Silk floss is expensive, but the subtle glow of coloured silks adds a touch of luxury to your work.

Viscose threads

Rayon viscose thread is available in several weights, on spools or in skeins. It is sometimes tricky to handle but the high-gloss finish adds a touch of glamour to any project.

Coton à broder

This fine, twisted thread has a matt finish and may not be separated into strands. It is very easy to use, defining stitches neatly, and suitable for small to medium projects.

Pearl cotton

This twisted, rounded thread is heavier than cotton floss and the strands may not be separated. Again, a wide range of colours is available in several weights: no. 5 is the most common, while no. 3 is heavier, and no. 8 and no. 12 are finer. Use pearl cotton for bold embroidery on medium to large projects.

Metallic threads

Many different types of metallic threads are available for hand embroidery, adding sparkle to your work.

TRY IT

83 *Can I use hand embroidery threads for machine embroidery?*

As a rule, hand embroidery threads are too heavy for machine stitching, but you can experiment with this technique:

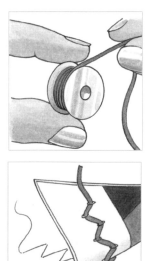

1 Wind a fairly heavy thread such as coton à broder or pearl cotton no. 8 or 12 onto a spare bobbin, making sure you wind in the same direction as the machine-wound process. Insert the bobbin in the machine and choose a matching or contrasting machine sewing thread for the upper thread.

2 Set the machine for zigzag stitch, at a fairly loose tension. Stitch slowly with the wrong side of the work uppermost, so the heavy thread appears on the right side. If necessary, draw guidelines with an erasable fabric marker. Experiment with different thread tension settings and stitch lengths: a very loose top thread tension will cause the heavy bobbin thread to pull the upper thread through the fabric in little loops, making a spiky line.

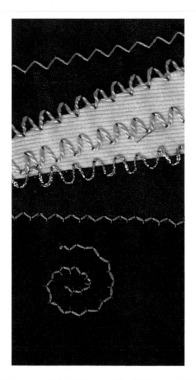

IN STITCHES

This section features both functional and decorative hand and machine stitches. Troubleshooting suggestions are given for when things go wrong and advice on finding the best stitch for the task in hand. Machine embroidery tips are offered here, with help for both freehand enthusiasts and digitized machine embroidery. Sergers (overlockers) – which sew seams and neaten raw edges all in one – are covered, including details on how they can be used for attractive decorative finishes as well as practical seaming.

Sewing by hand

Hand sewing is still important even in this modern world of machines and gadgets. Great satisfaction can be achieved from producing beautiful hand sewing and embroidery.

84

Nine
WAYS TO PERFECT HAND STITCHES

1 Pin or baste
Before you start to stitch, hold seams and hems securely and accurately in place with pins or basting.

2 Sit comfortably
Sit in good light, with a window or light source behind your left shoulder (if you are right-handed). Hold the work in your lap. When working on large or heavy articles, sit at a table, with the bulk of the work supported on the table top.

3 Thread length
A long thread has a tendency to knot or tangle, whereas a shorter length is more easily controlled.

4 Use silk
If you have a choice, choose silk. Silk thread slips nicely through the fabric and any knots that may form fall out easily.

5 Needle know-how
To make the job easier, choose an appropriate needle for each task. A small betweens needle is ideal for small, neat stitches, while a large-eyed needle is a must for thicker embroidery thread.

6 Even stitches
Stitches must be consistent in their size and regularly spaced. This makes them strong and neat.

7 Clean work
Don't forget to wash your hands frequently when sewing. Hot, sweaty hands can make fabric and threads grimy. If you are working on a long project, keep it wrapped in cotton sheeting between sewing sessions. A duvet cover acts as a handy protective bag when sewing a large bridal gown.

8 Knotty start
It doesn't matter whether you start sewing with a knot or a double stitch as long as it is secure. Remember to finish work with two or more stitches in the same place to ensure the thread doesn't come undone.

9 Thread too short
When the thread becomes shorter than the needle, put the needle in the fabric, then place the thread end through the eye and pull the needle to the wrong side.

TRY IT

85 *Should I use a thimble?*

A thimble protects your finger when hand sewing and allows the needle to be pushed through stubborn layers of fabric when necessary. Choose one that fits well and sits comfortably on your middle finger.

• Traditional thimble
These are normally metal (but sometimes plastic) and dimpled so that the back of the needle sits in a hollow to prevent it from slipping when it is pushed through fabric.

• Leather quilting thimble
Soft and flexible, leather thimbles often have side vents to make them less hot and more comfortable and also have a metal insert to help push the needle through.

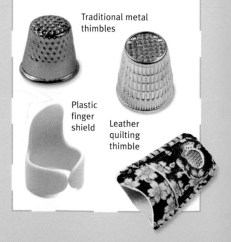

Traditional metal thimbles

Plastic finger shield

Leather quilting thimble

86

Essential hand stitches

There are just a few vital hand stitches that can be used for many tasks. Learn these and you will be able to complete any sewing project safe in the knowledge that it will secure the fabric where you want it.

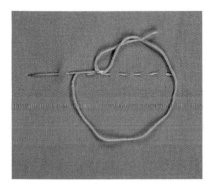

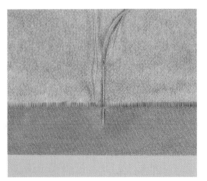

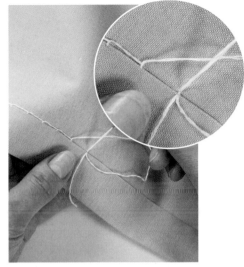

Running stitch

How? This simple stitch is formed by taking the needle up and down through the cloth, making regularly spaced, even stitches.

Where? Use this stitch for a seam to join fabrics together.

Hem stitch

How? Make a row of tiny diagonal stitches to hold up a folded edge. The stitches catch a few threads of fabric, holding it securely in place.

Where? Hemming stitches are used to secure a hem. It is a strong stitch, but not necessarily invisible.

Lock stitch

How? Make a stitch about 12mm (¹⁄₂in) long, but before pulling the thread through, take the thread under the needle.

Where? Use this as a hemming stitch on garments and curtains.

The advantage of lock stitch is that if the thread breaks, the lock stitches on either side of the break will hold firm long enough for a repair to be made. With other hemming stitches, if a stitch is caught the thread gets completely pulled out.

Blanket stitch

How? Make stitches over the edge of a piece of cloth, catching each stitch before pulling the thread through so the stitches link together.

Where? These stitches neaten and strengthen an edge.

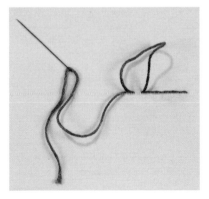

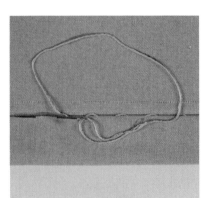

Backstitch

How? Make a small stitch down through the fabric and then up again. Take the needle back to fill in the gap. Continue forwards, making these regular stitches along the length.

Where? This stitch is perfect when a strong seam is required. It is especially useful as the seam then has a certain amount of stretch.

Slip stitch

How? Slide the needle through the folded edge and take a small stitch into the fabric opposite. Continue to take regular stitches along the length of the hem.

Where? Use slip stitching for an invisible hem.

(87)

Eight
WAYS TO PERFECT EMBROIDERY STITCHES

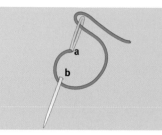

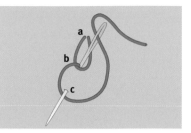

1 Hold the fabric flat

Keep the fabric taut while you stitch to prevent puckering. You can use an embroidery hoop and/or apply a suitable stabilizer to the right or wrong side of the work. Stabilizers (page 71) may be permanent or removable (peel-off, wash-away, or heat-soluble).

2 Draw guidelines

A design or guidelines may be drawn on the fabric surface with an erasable fabric marker, or drawn onto removable stabilizer applied to the right side of the fabric.

3 Start without a knot

Begin about 2.5cm (1in) away from where the first stitch will be. Leaving a thread tail of about 5cm (2in) on the surface, make two or three backstitches towards the starting point. Work the embroidery, then unpick the backstitches and run in the starting tail along the backs of the stitches, as 7.

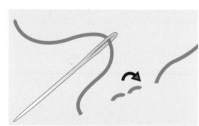

Start without a knot

Finish neatly

4 Chain stitch

1 Bring the needle up at **a**, form a loop with the thread and insert the needle back at **a**, bringing it out at **b**, inside the loop. Pull through gently (do not over-tighten).
2 Form another loop with the thread and insert the needle at **b**, bringing it out at **c**, inside the new loop. Pull through.
3 Repeat as required. All stitches should be the same length. Secure the last loop with a tiny stitch.

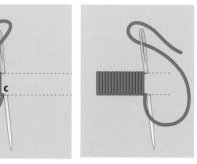

5 Satin stitch

Bring the needle up at **a**, down at **b** and up at **c**. Repeat as required. Stitches should be close together and parallel, with no gaps between them, giving a solid band of colour with the stitches.

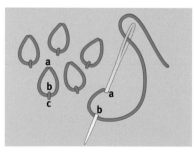

6 Lazy daisy stitch

Bring the needle up at **a** and form a loop with the thread. Insert the needle again at **a** and bring it out at **b**, inside the loop. Pull through gently. Insert the needle at **c**, outside the loop of thread.

Finished lazy daisy flower

7 Finish neatly

Once you have some embroidery stitches in place, all the other thread tails may be run in along the backs of the stitches.

8 Press correctly

Don't over-press hand embroidery, or the stitches will be flattened. Lay the work right side down on a thick, soft layer (such as a folded towel) and press gently.

French knots

These are great for adding texture to a design. Mounting the fabric in an embroidery hoop will make this stitch much easier to work.

1 Wrap the thread round the needle. Take the needle to the wrong side, holding the looped thread on the right side at the same time.

2 Bring the needle back up at the same point and through the loop in the thread.

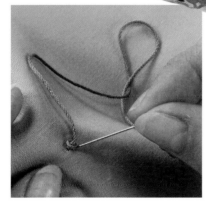

3 To fasten the stitch, take the needle over the loop and through to the wrong side. Neaten securely at the back.

FIX IT

89 *How do I mend a hole?*

Darning and patching are not commonly used techniques today but knowing how to repair a hole or a worn area of cloth might just be what you need to prolong the life of a favourite garment.

To darn, use colour-matching thread to make parallel stitches across the hole or worn area. Extend into the good cloth to get a secure hold and weave up and down through the fabric with a running stitch. Repeat with more stitches perpendicular to the first ones. This strengthens and fills the worn fabric.

Darning: back view.

Front view

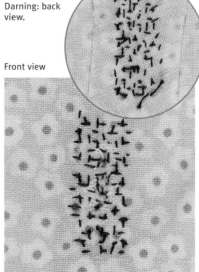

Patching is a good alternative to darning. Where a damaged area of fabric is too large to darn, cut a patch of fabric to cover it entirely. Use a colour-matching fabric or a contrast. Tuck under the raw edges and place the patch over the hole. Hand stitch in place with hemming stitches.

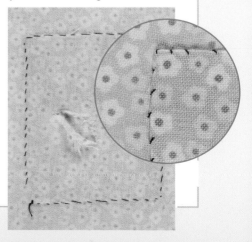

MAKE IT!

Book cover

Make a cover for a diary, address book or recipe book with a simple needlepoint panel.

You will need:
- Felt, to fit book
- Sewing equipment: water-soluble fabric pen, tape measure, scissors, pins, sharp sewing needle, sewing thread for basting
- Ruler and set square
- Sharp needle

- Pearl cotton: about 7.2m (8yd) to complement the felt and the embroidery
- Embroidered samples; ours is a tapestry strawberry measuring 5 x 5cm (2 x 2in)

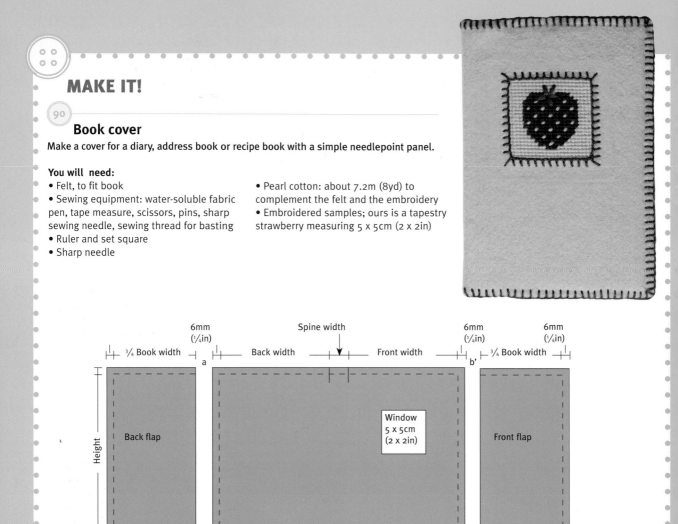

1 Measure the book with a tape measure. Use a ruler, set square and water-soluble fabric pen to draw the outlines onto the felt, matching your measurements and adding 6mm (¼in) seam allowances on the pattern above. To ensure your drawing is accurately square, the two diagonals a–a' and b–b' should both measure exactly the same. Draw a window: ours measures 5 x 5cm (2 x 2in) and is at the centre of the front panel, 3cm (1¼in) from the top.

2 Cut out the pieces. Pin the embroidery behind the window, matching the edges carefully. Baste all around with sewing thread. Use a sharp needle and pearl cotton to work blanket stitch (page 59) all around the edge of the window, covering the raw edge of the felt. Use the canvas mesh beneath to keep the stitches an even size: ours were two holes deep and two holes apart. At each corner, work three stitches in the same place. Remove the basting.

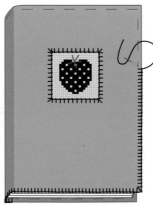

3 Pin the cover in position with the book closed. Baste the edges together all around. Use the sharp needle and pearl cotton to work blanket stitch all around the outside edge, through both layers of felt, matching the size of the stitches to those around the window. Work three stitches into the same place at each corner. Hide the thread ends between the felt layers. Remove the basting. Mist with water to remove traces of the water-soluble fabric pen and allow to dry.

Magical machine stitches

Modern machines do all sorts of stitches and make sewing tasks quicker and easier. Most machines will also do at least a small number of decorative stitches, while some can produce complicated embroidery designs. Whatever machine you are using, make sure you are getting the best from it.

91 Stretch stitch

Although a narrow zigzag stitch can be set on even the most basic sewing machine, a dedicated stretch stitch is useful for sewing knitted and stretchy fabrics.

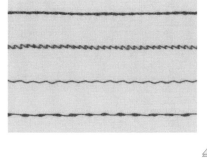

- Try out the stretch stitch options on scraps of fabric to see which is most suitable for the fabric (see right).

- A stretch stitch can cause the fabric edge to ripple or become wavy. To avoid this, use the stitch in conjunction with a walking foot.

92 Top tension tips

Most modern electronic sewing machines have automatic tension, which need not be adjusted. If the tension has to be altered, take a note of the settings before doing so and adjust only the needle tension. The bobbin tension should only be changed by an experienced mechanic.

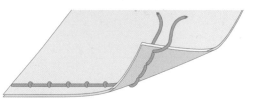

Imagine a cross-sectional view through the fabric and stitch. The upper and lower threads meet in the middle of the fabric and link to form the stitches. The sewing machine is set up so that the stitches made by the needle thread, which appear on the surface, have a better appearance than those formed by the bobbin thread. For this reason, when machine gathering, always pull the bobbin thread as this will slide through the fabric more easily.

If either the upper or lower thread is straight with the opposite one doing all the stitch formation, there is a tension problem (see above). Sew out a row of stitching on a double layer of fabric to check.

For decorative stitching, where a thicker thread is used in the bobbin, buy a separate bobbin holder. Adjust the tension on one bobbin holder, keeping the original for regular stitching.

FIX IT

93 *How do I fix loopy or tight stitches, breaking thread and skipped stitches?*

- Use the same thread in the needle and in the bobbin for regular stitching. If different threads are used, the tension may be troublesome.

- Check the thread route to the needle. Occasionally the thread slips out of the guides or tension discs and this will affect the tension. On many modern machines the thread route is concealed by the body of the machine, which means that problems like this are difficult to identify.

- Remove the bobbin from the shuttle/bobbin case. Dust away any lint build-up or remove trapped threads and replace the bobbin.

- Clean the tension discs (if accessible) by knotting a length of thread several times and pulling it back and forth through the discs.

- Check the needle. Replace it if there is any indication that it may be blunt, bent or the wrong type for the fabric (see page 14). Make sure that the new needle is pushed fully into place and is secured well.

Blind hem stitch, placed along a folded edge, will pull a soft, silky fabric into a shell formation. This hem works particularly well on bias-cut edges.

94

Soft shell edge

This easy-to-sew technique is made with a blind hem stitch over the edge of a soft, lightweight fabric like chiffon. It produces a pretty finish suitable for hemming scarves. It can also be used to neaten the edges on medium- and heavier-weight fabrics, but the scalloped or shell edge will not be apparent. Instead, a straight neat edge will be produced which looks particularly good when sewn with a contrasting thread.

1 Press a 6mm (¼ in) seam allowance to the wrong side.

2 Fit a standard presser foot and select a blind hem stitch.

3 On a scrap piece of fabric, try out the stitch to check the effect created. Sew the main stitches on the fabric but allow the needle to miss the fabric on the 'swing' stitch. It is the 'swing' stitch that pulls the fabric in to form a scallop. To alter the shell-shaped edge, lengthen or shorten the stitch length and width and increase the tension. When satisfied with the edge finish produced, create the effect along the edge of the chosen fabric.

95

Neat tips

• Cut with sharp pinking shears before turning under the seam allowance to prevent ravelling.
• Use a fine, metallic thread for a subtle, glittery edge.
• Pivot carefully at the corners, or sew each edge independently and neaten the thread ends by sewing in with a hand needle on the wrong side.

A blind hem stitch sits over the edge of a firm fabric while on chiffon, a shell edge is produced.

96

Three-step zigzag or tricot stitch

A three-step variation of a zigzag, it forms a flat, wide zigzag stitch without pulling up or curling the fabric under it as an ordinary zigzag might do. It is especially useful for attaching elastic for lingerie or swimwear.

To attach the elastic, divide it into four equal sections. Do the same with the fabric then re-pin, matching the pins through both layers. Lengthen the stitch and sew, stretching the elastic to fit the fabric so that when the elastic relaxes, the fabric sits evenly.

Teflon foot used when stitching clear elastic to prevent sticking – not necessary when stitching cotton fabrics.

1 Set the sewing machine to sew three-step zigzag and increase the stitch length. Place the fabric, with the right side up, and the elastic on top and adjacent to the edge. Lower the needle and presser foot and sew a few stitches to secure the end. Hold the fabric and elastic at the back with your left hand, and pull gently on the elastic with your right. Continue to sew. The elastic will pull the fabric up into gathers.

2 Fold the elastic to the wrong side and sew a new row of three-step zigzag from the right side through all layers below. Pull gently to extend the elastic and fabric as you sew. This row of stitching keeps the elastic to the wrong side and makes a neat finish.

TRY IT

97 *What's the best way to decorate a plain skirt?*

Try adding horizontal rows of decorative stitching to the hem edge. Choose simple straight stitches and zigzags in interesting colours, or use variegated threads. Depending on what is available on your machine, select more interesting leaf, flower or star designs.

For a distinctive effect, try thicker thread or crochet yarn, which, although too thick to be threaded through the eye of a needle, can be wound onto the bobbin. With a standard thread in the needle, sew with the fabric upside down. This creates a strong decorative stitch on the right side of the fabric. Do not alter the tension on the machine's bobbin holder. Keep a separate bobbin holder for this purpose.

Sew with thick variegated thread in the bobbin.

98

Scalloped edge

This decorative stitch makes a pretty edge for an antique style or the hem of a little girl's dress.

- Take care to sew steadily to make the stitches regular. Erratic speed may cause the scallops to vary in size.

- Adjust the stitch width and length for a good scallop shape with dense thread coverage.

- On a delicate fabric, use a layer of wash-away stabilizer under the edge to support the stitches.

- Use a suitable presser foot for decorative stitching.

1 Sew a row of scalloped stitches 2.5cm (1in) from the edge.

2 Carefully trim away the fabric from the outside edge without snipping the thread of the stitches.

Buttonholes

Whether your machine offers one or a choice of buttonholes (plain, tailored keyhole, stretch fabric, and so on), garments can be finished much more quickly and will look more professional than when hand sewn – if that is what you want.

100

Ten

TIPS FOR CREATING THE BEST BUTTONHOLES

1 Use a double layer of fabric. For stretch, lightweight, or loosely woven fabrics, use a tear-away or wash-away stabilizer to support the work when sewing.

2 Choose a suitable buttonhole for the task: narrow, broad, keyhole, bound or hand finished.

3 Practise making the buttonhole on scrap fabric first to see what it looks like and to ensure the size is appropriate for your chosen buttons.

4 Sew the least prominent buttonhole first and work towards the most prominent.

5 Use a fine needle.

6 Place a pin across the end of the buttonhole to avoid cutting too far when opening the buttonhole.

7 Use silk organza as a stabilizer when sewing a button onto sheer fabric. It will help to anchor it.

8 Rather than sewing a running stitch as a guide for a hand-worked buttonhole, machine sew the parallel lines.

9 For tailored (keyhole) buttonholes, use a punch to remove a neat hole at one end before stitching.

10 For vertical buttons, sew bars at both ends instead of making one round end.

99

Simple buttonholes

When a machine doesn't offer a dedicated buttonhole stitch, follow this sequence.

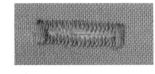

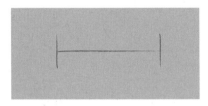

1 Mark the position and length of the buttonhole with a temporary marker pen.

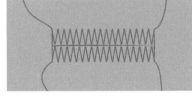

2 Set the sewing machine to a narrow satin stitch, width 2mm (¹⁄₁₆in) and length 4mm (¹⁄₈in). Test the stitch to find the right size for the task. Sew two parallel lines to form the edges of the buttonhole.

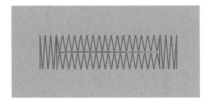

3 Double the stitch width and sew bars at either end of the buttonhole, or thread the tails onto a needle and sew the bars by hand to finish the ends of the buttonhole.

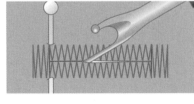

4 Cut the buttonhole open with a seam ripper. Place a pin at one end to protect the bar, and cut towards it. Alternatively, use a buttonhole chisel (see page 29).

101

Shaped buttonholes

Many embroidery machines offer the chance to sew buttonholes in a frame. These buttonhole designs range from basic styles with straight or rounded ends to more ornate and decorative shapes. The advantage of them being sewn in a frame is that a very neat finish can be produced.

102

Hand worked buttonhole

In theory, there is no need to work buttonholes by hand these days as those produced by machine are strong, neat and very quick to make. However, it may be necessary to understand how they are sewn for making traditional clothing designs or historic costumes.

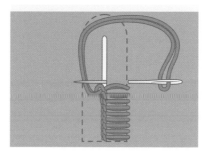

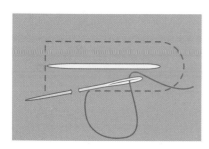

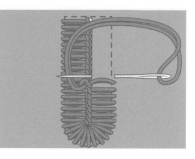

1 Mark the position of the buttonhole and cut it open. Hand sew a row of running stitches on each side of the slash, and round one end 2mm (¹⁄₁₆in) from it. This holds the layers of fabric together and acts as a guide for the size of the stitches.

2 Use a double thread (drawn through beeswax). Hold the buttonhole vertically and secure the thread end at the bottom of the slash. With the fabric in the left hand, work the right edge of the slash, sewing upwards with close and even buttonhole stitches.

3 Stitch around the end and turn the work around, before sewing up the other side.

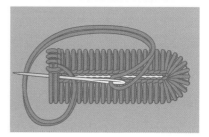

4 Finish the buttonhole with a bar made with two or three threads and covered with buttonhole stitches.

103

Machine-bound buttonhole

In a bound buttonhole, fabric (rather than stitches) covers the edges of the slit. Depending on the look required for the garment, it can be made with matching or contrasting fabric. Methods of construction vary, but this way is easy and produces a strong finish. For extra support, fuse interfacing to the wrong side of the fabric.

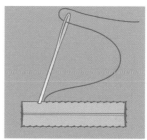

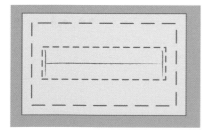

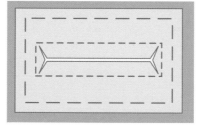

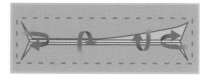

3 Pull the fabric through the hole and tug out the ends. Manipulate the fabric to lie flat over the lips created by the raw edges inside. Prick stitch in the ditch to hold the buttonhole in place. Press flat.

1 Place a bias-cut piece of fabric on the surface of the fabric and baste in place. Mark the position and shape of the buttonhole, shorten the stitch length and then sew around the shape. (Start in the middle rather than at a corner for added strength.)

2 Cut through the centre of the buttonhole and close into the corners without snipping the threads.

4 Mark the position of the buttonhole on the facing and cut through the centre and into the corners. Press the raw edges under and sew in place at the back of the buttonhole.

Machine embroidery

Machine embroidery is created either freehand or by using digitizing software. The techniques are completely different, with the first requiring artistic skill to produce the design and the latter needing less skill to stitch out the design but just as much creativity in its preparation, plus some computer knowledge.

With a little patience and colourful threads, freehand embroidery can create some truly exotic results.

Machine embroidery is perfect if you have a pattern you wish to tessellate, as in the decorative border below.

104

Freehand versus machine embroidery

Freehand embroidery

Use a standard sewing machine with the feed dogs dropped out of use. Move the fabric (often held taut in a hoop) under the needle to form a design. The faster you move the fabric, the longer the stitch, so practice and control are needed for good results. This is often called 'painting with stitches'.

Machine embroidery

You will need a computerized sewing machine that stitches out a digitized design. You can create a design with software or use designs available on the Internet, purchased on a card, or transferred via a memory stick. The design can be resized, rotated and positioned before being stitched out. Less artistic ability is required to stitch out the design, but you must monitor it and change the thread as required.

105

Ten

TIPS FOR SUCCESSFUL MACHINE EMBROIDERY

1 Use the correct stabilizer for the task.

2 Wind bobbin fill (extra fine thread) onto the bobbin. Because it is so fine, it allows the quality embroidery thread to look its best on the surface. It is also more economical, saving the need to fill with matching embroidery thread. A longer length can be wound onto the bobbin, meaning fewer bobbin changes.

3 Use a good quality needle and change it frequently.

4 Fit fabric into the hoop carefully, following the instructions and matching any symbols.

5 Hoop fabric tightly without stretching.

6 Use a sticky stabilizer, or a temporary adhesive, with a stretch fabric to fully support it.

7 Do not hoop delicate fabrics that will be damaged when clamped. Hoop a standard stabilizer, spray with temporary adhesive and position fabric over the hoop, sticking it in place.

8 Mark the position of the design with basting stitches or a temporary marking pen. When the fabric or garment is in position in the hoop, it can look very different.

9 Remove jump threads by snipping with curved scissors to prevent them from being trapped under other stitches.

10 Use clear, wash-away stabilizer over the surface of towelling and pile fabrics. The final embroidered design sits on the fabric and does not get lost within the loops.

Place fabric in the hoop or frame before stitching out.

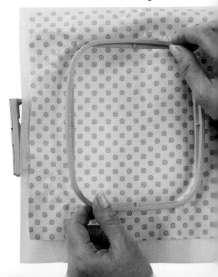

What to look for when buying an embroidery machine

Dedicated or combination?

Some machines are designed only for embroidery, while others also function as a standard sewing machine. Combination machines take up less storage space than two machines. However, it can sometimes be useful to have an embroidery machine set up alongside a standard sewing machine so that work can be carried out more quickly.

Hoop size

More expensive sewing machines have a larger sewing area. This makes it possible to stitch out a bigger design or to join several smaller pieces together without rehooping the fabric. Conversely, a larger hoop needs more fabric and stabilizer, which may be wasteful for a small design. Consider how you intend to use the embroidery machine and therefore what hoop size will be most appropriate.

Transferring the design

Embroidery machines have some designs built into the memory but new ones can be imported in a variety of ways. Some require a card specific to the manufacturer but most up-to-date models have a USB port. If you do not intend to create your own designs, choose a machine with a good store of built-in designs and with more designs commercially available.

Speed

Stitch speed can vary between machines and models. If you need to work quickly, choose one that imports designs quickly and has a high stitch speed.

Display

In general, the more expensive the machine the easier it is to lay out and edit the design on the screen. A large colour screen makes moving and adjusting the design much easier.

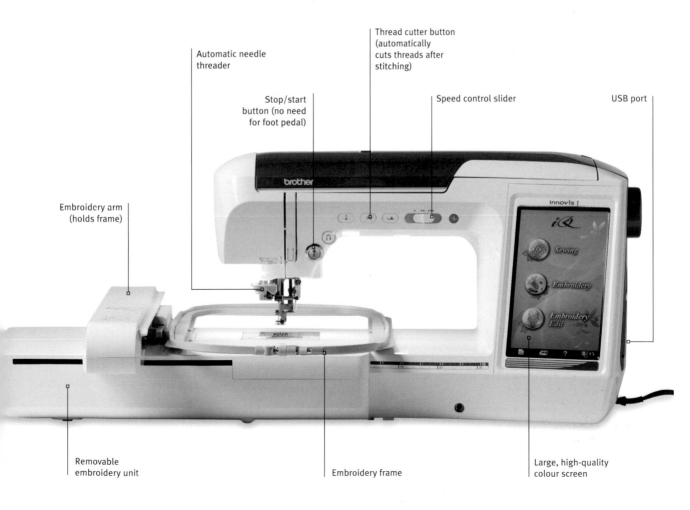

Automatic needle threader

Thread cutter button (automatically cuts threads after stitching)

Stop/start button (no need for foot pedal)

Speed control slider

USB port

Embroidery arm (holds frame)

Removable embroidery unit

Embroidery frame

Large, high-quality colour screen

(107)

Machine embroidered stitch designs

There are various functions on your embroidery machine – most notably the stitch width dial – that will present you with myriad design choices. The following examples will inspire you to get creative.

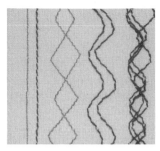 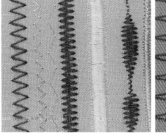 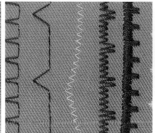 

Straight stitching

Thread the machine and insert the bobbin in the normal way. Using the standard embroidery presser foot, experiment with different types of thread and different stitch lengths. Work stitches in spaced or overlapping rows or mass lines of stitchery to cover the background surface.

Zigzag and satin stitching

By adjusting the stitch width dial, various widths of stitch can be achieved. This is used in conjunction with the stitch length dial. For example, a wide satin stitch requires the highest number stitch width and the lowest stitch length.

Automatic stitching

Prepare the machine as for zigzag stitching with a wide stitch width and a low number stitch length. Select an automatic embroidery stitch, test on scrap fabric for effect and then proceed, using a variety of decorative stitches in rows.

Experimental stitching

Experiment with different types of thread, and vary the length and width of the stitches.

TRY IT

(108) *How do you embroider flowers freehand?*

Decorate a hat or bag with some freehand flowers by following these simple steps.

1 Draw the outline of a simple flower shape on a piece of stiff interfacing or stablizer.

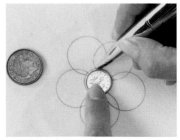

Use coins or buttons for petal shapes, outlining with a wash-away or fade-away pen.

2 Drop the feed dogs on the sewing machine and set for straight stitch.

3 Fit a darning foot to the machine.

4 Stitch in a circular motion to fill each petal in turn with stitches. Cover the petal area entirely.

5 Change thread colour and create the centre of the flower in the same way.

6 Trim away the stabilizer from the edge of the flower close to the stitches.

7 Raise the feed dogs and replace the darning foot with a standard one. Stitch a satin stitch around the flower to define the edge.

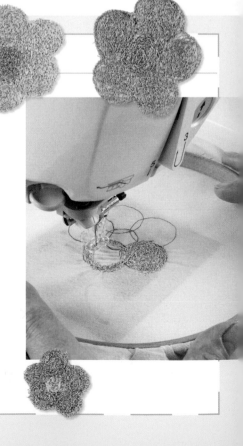

(109)

Stabilizer options

A stabilizer is essential to support fabric while stitching and to improve the finished result. Stabilizers come in all weights and types to suit all fabrics and tasks.

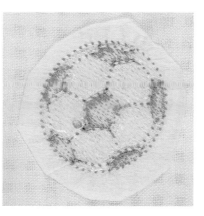

Cut-away

Available in various weights, cut-aways are placed under the design while it is being stitched, to support and cushion it. Simply place the stabilizer to the wrong side of the fabric and fit into the frame.

The excess is cut away when the embroidery is completed. Suitable for logos on T-shirts and sweatshirts, or on garments that are finished with a lining.

Clear film

Used on the surface of a pile fabric in combination with a standard stabilizer underneath the fabric, clear film is removed once the embroidery is complete by washing or with a hot iron. Suitable for towelling and velvet, or for making lace where the clear stabilizer is hooped and the design stitched directly to it. The stabilizer is washed away when the design is complete.

Adhesive stabilizers

Some sticky stabilizers have a backing that is removed to reveal the adhesive surface; others are ironed to the fabric so the heat holds the stabilizer in place. For most convenient use, stretch the stabilizer with a backing into the hoop and then score with a pin. This allows you to peel away the protective backing. Useful for small pieces of fabric, garments not large enough to fit into a hoop and stretch fabrics that will distort when pulled into a hoop.

Tear away

As above, place to the wrong side of the fabric and fit into the frame before stitching out the design. The excess stabilizer tears away easily, reducing bulk at the back of the design, and eliminating

any crinkles around the embroidery on the right side. Ideal for embroidered skirts, shirts, tablewear and pillows.

Serging ahead

For a neat and tidy finish and a professional appearance, a serger is an essential tool in the sewing room. As well as very effective seams and neat edges, a serger produces a variety of creative finishes.

110

How does a serger work?

Unlike a sewing machine, a serger operates with one or two needles and two loopers. A blade cuts off excess fabric from the seam, and the loopers and threads work together to sew the seam and form stitches over the raw edge.

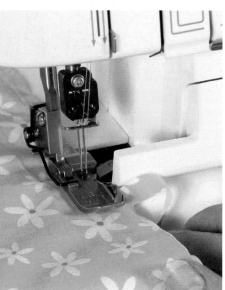

111

How to choose a serger

When buying a serger for the first time, people often choose the cheapest one available, with the idea of replacing it with a more expensive model if they decide serging is for them. Sadly this often leads to disappointment, as cheaper models are more difficult to thread and use in comparison to better-made, more costly models. There are three main things to consider.

Three or four threads?

A three-thread machine will neaten edges and may do some other creative finishes but has less scope than a four-thread machine, which will operate as a three-thread machine as well anyway. Go for four if you can.

Cover stitch

Some sergers offer a cover stitch function that produces a surface serging stitch in addition to the edge stitching. These machines can use up to eight threads but they are quite complicated to thread and use. If you are serious about serging, and have time to spend learning how to use the machine to its full potential, then buy one.

Easy threading

Choose a serger with easy threading. Many hours can be wasted threading up that could otherwise be spent sewing. Some models offer a very easy-to-operate air-threading system, and if this is within your budget consider it seriously.

Three-thread serging

Four-thread serging

112

Advance knowledge

If there are local instructors offering classes on serger sewing, attend a class before you buy a machine. You will get support in using the machine while learning more about it. And, if serging is for you, you will have a better idea of the functions you will need when buying your own.

FIX IT

113 *Why do the threads keep breaking?*

To prevent threads from snapping, thread the serger in the correct order (as shown right). Ideally, thread the upper looper first, then the lower looper, and finally the needles. If a looper thread breaks, it is important to snip the needle threads. Rethread them only after rerouting the looper thread.

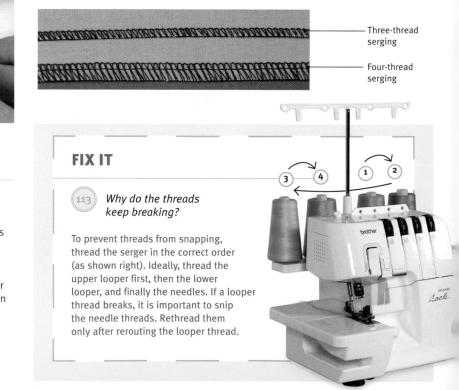

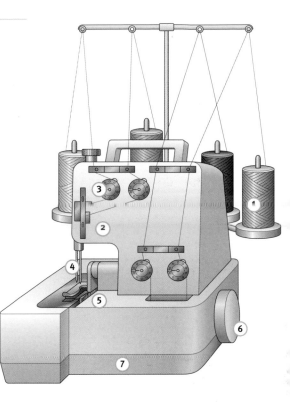

(114)

Anatomy of a serger

These have become very popular in recent years as they allow home sewers to benefit from a manufactured seam finish. They also produce wonderful creative seams and edges, and sew modern stretch fabrics with ease.

1 Thread spindles

There are four of these on most sergers. The two on the left feed the needles and the two on the right feed the loopers.

2 Thread guides

These hold the threads in the correct routes before reaching the needles and loopers.

3 Tension dials

These allow the threads to be adjusted and so form different types of stitch, for example, a balanced stitch, flatlocking and rolled hemming.

4 Needles

There are normally two needles on a serger. They may both be used for four-thread serging. Wide three-thread serging is made with the left needle in position. Narrow serging uses the right needle only.

5 Knives

The knives cut off the excess fabric before the threads form stitches over the cut edge.

6 Fly wheel

The fly wheel or balance wheel can be turned by hand to raise or lower the needles.

7 Loopers

The loopers (not visible on the diagram shown) feed the threads below the needles and allow stitches to be formed when they link with the needle threads.

FIX IT

(115) *How do you fix loose loops or pulled threads?*

Most sergers work by feeding the threads through tension dials. The threads are released at the correct tension to allow a perfect balanced stitch to be formed with the links right on the edge of the cut cloth. If you are experiencing tension problems, follow these suggestions:

- Is each thread lying in its correct route or have any slipped out of any of the guides?

- The threads can easily jump out of the tension dials. Look at each dial and make sure that each thread is lying between the tension discs. Pull the thread carefully through the discs and check there is some, but not too much, resistance.

- Are the threads used in the needle(s) and loopers all the same? If different types or thicknesses of threads are used, the stitches may not link as they should.

- Are the needles both the same size? Although not directly connected to tension, the needle can cause missed stitches and unbalanced stitching.

Often an older needle becomes dull or blunt and this can affect the stitch quality. If in any doubt, change one or both.

- Have the tension dials been moved accidentally? If so, return them to their normal positions.

- The tension dials can sometimes get dirty with lint and residue from the threads. Knot a length of thread several times in the middle and pull this back and forth through the dials to clean them.

If none of the above helps improve the stitch quality, it is time to adjust the tension dials (see page 74 for details). If this doesn't work, then seek assistance.

116

Essential creative serging techniques

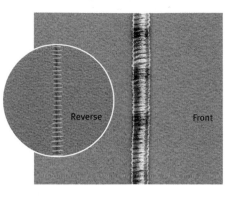

Reverse   Front

Flatlocking

This decorative serging joins two pieces of fabric with a flat seam. It is sewn with two or three threads depending on the model. Use flatlocking for sportswear. Refer to the manual for specific instructions or follow these guidelines, making adjustments to achieve the best result for the fabric.

- Use either left or right needle.

- Set the needle tension to zero.

- Tighten the lower looper tension.

- Use a standard stitch length.

- Feed the fabric under the blade and needle with wrong sides together and serge the seam. Pull flat to allow the loops of the seam to lie on the top.

Rolled hemming

Rolled hemming uses three threads. The lower looper tension is tightened and the upper looper tension loosened so that the upper threads wrap tightly over the edge, covering it entirely. Use rolled hemming on edges and hems for a delicate finish. Refer to the manual for specific instructions or follow these guidelines, making adjustments to achieve the best result for the fabric.

- Remove the left needle.

- Remove the 'stitch finger' over which normal stitches are formed.

- Shorten the stitch length.

- Tighten the lower looper tension.

- Loosen the upper looper tension.

- Lengthen the stitch length for a picot edge; pull the fabric slightly when stitching to create a lettuce edge (see opposite); stitch over the nylon fishing line and spread the finished hem along the line to give a fluted edge (see page 150).

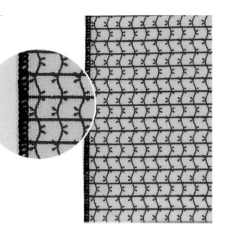

117

How to test tension

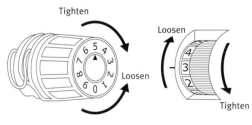

Tighten

Loosen

Loosen

Loosen

Tighten

- Write down the tension dial numbers before adjusting them.

- Use four colours of the same type of thread and sew a test length of serging.

- Take a good look at the stitches. The upper and lower threads should meet on the edge and the fabric beneath the stitches should be flat with no overhanging loops.

- If any of the threads appear to be too tight or they are too loose, turn the dials to correct the problem. The higher the number, the greater the tension or pull on the thread; the lower the number, the less drag on the thread.

- Adjust, test, examine, readjust, retest and examine again until the stitches are perfectly balanced.

FIX IT

118 *Why do my flatlock stitches disappear at the seam?*

Flatlocking is an ideal method for seaming knits, as it stretches with the fabric. However, if the ends of the seam are not finished securely, or if the seam is cut by another seam, the threads may pull and unravel, making the seam fall apart. To prevent this from happening, tie off the thread tails securely.

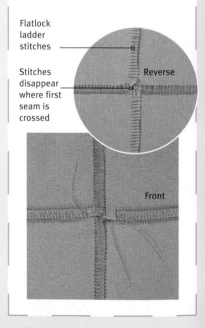

Flatlock ladder stitches

Stitches disappear where first seam is crossed

Reverse

Front

119
Making a lettuce hem

For a pretty frilled hem, neaten with a lettuce edge. Simply set the serger to rolled hemming (see page 72) and feed the fabric under the presser foot, pulling the fabric edge slightly in front and behind the needle and foot. This places more stitches onto the edge, making it curl.

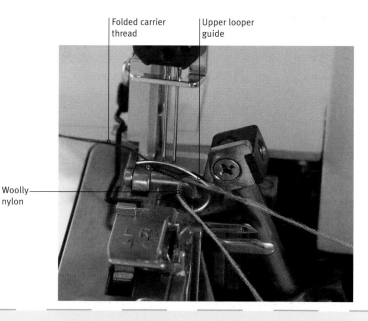

Four- or six-ply variegated threads by Madeira give a very attractive effect that is softer than a solid colour.

120
Can I use fancy or novelty threads?

Because loopers have a larger hole than a needle, it is possible to produce creative serging with thicker fancy and novelty threads. For most decorative effects, route these threads through the upper looper, although the lower looper can also be used.

Woolly nylon or floss gives a good coverage and is great for seams and flatlocking.

If spun evenly, crochet cotton, pearl cotton or yarn gives a bold edge.

Metallic threads – thick or thin – produce a pretty hem for evening wear or scarves.

FIX IT

121 Can I thread thick yarn using my serger?

Use a 'carrier thread' to thread thick yarns through the serger loops and guides. Take a standard thread about 60cm (24in) long and fold it in half. Thread the cut ends together through the guides, carrying the thicker yarn with it.

Folded carrier thread

Upper looper guide

Woolly nylon

SEWING TECHNIQUES

Although the most obvious way to join pieces of fabric together is to sew a plain seam, there are other alternatives more suitable for particular types of fabric and seam positions. Shape can be introduced through seaming, making darts, gathering and pleating. In this chapter you will find techniques for finishing hems and edges, and tips for adding pockets of various styles to garments and bags. The inside secrets of interfacings and underlinings are also covered, along with helpful suggestions for linings. All in all, this chapter will answer your sewing techniques queries, making it fun and easy.

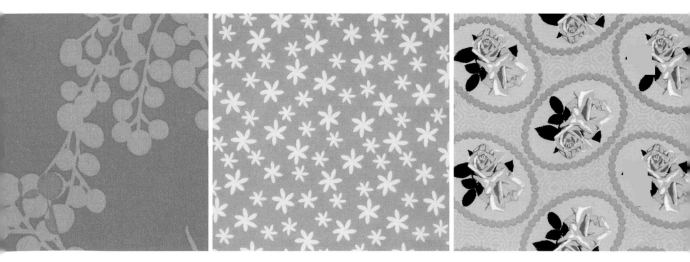

Using paper patterns

Commercial paper patterns are available for all types of sewing, from dressmaking and costumes to soft furnishings and crafts. Most of the pattern companies follow an international sizing code as well as using similar pattern markings and terminology.

122

Reading the pattern envelope

1 Image of the finished garment(s)

This indicates what the finished item will look like. Normally, there are variations of a style: short and long sleeve options, or different collar choices, for example. Be aware that photographs give a more accurate illustration of the finished garment. Drawings may have a designer's licence, showing tall, slim figures and may not represent how the finished garment will look on a smaller, rounder figure.

2 Size

The pattern will have a size printed on it whether it is a multisized pattern (in sizes 10–20); a single size (6); or a small range (12, 14 and 16). There will also be a size chart on the envelope stating the standard measurement for each size. Choose the most appropriate and adapt as necessary.

3 Description

A short description explains the details of the designs included in the envelope.

4 Notions

Any extra requirements needed to complete the garment are included on the back of the envelope: a zip and its length, and the number and suggested size of buttons, for example.

5 Fabrics

A number of suggestions for suitable fabrics to choose from is given, along with the amount of fabric required.

6 Back view

The back of the garment will normally be illustrated as a small diagram or line drawing showing details such as pocket positions, closures and seams. Front views may also be illustrated in a diagram.

7 Garment details

Specific information about the design is often printed on the back of the envelope. For trousers, for example, it may state the circumference of the leg at the hem or the side length from the waist. This gives a better indication of the fit and style, before you start to sew.

8 Other information

The company name and a pattern identification number are always stated on the front of the envelope. Sometimes the level of skill required to make up the pattern – whether the construction is easy or difficult – is stated on the envelope. The general fit of the style is often included, indicating whether the style may be 'loose fitting' or 'close fit'.

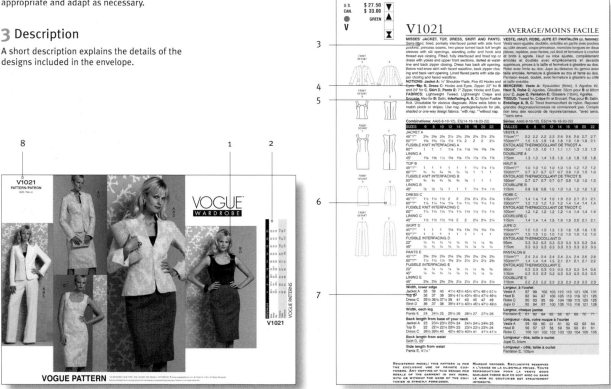

123

Fitting your garment

All patterns have an allowance for 'fit or wearing ease' and may also have a 'designer' ease. The amount contributes to the finished size and whether the garment is meant to be close or loose fitting. The wearing ease is the amount of 'wriggle' room added; thus a close-fitting bodice will have very little, while a coat will have enough to enable it to be worn over a jacket. The designer ease is the fashion ease, the extra fullness the designer builds in to create the silhouette-shape required.

As a guideline, the following allowances are frequently used:
Knit-fit: Very close (garment measures at or under body measurement).
Close fit: Very close, 3–6mm (¼–½in) ease.
Fitted: Garment contours closely to body.
Semi-fitted Garment skims the figure, following body shape.
Relaxed/loose fit: An 'easy' fit with 14–18cm (5½–7in) allowance for tops or 10–14cm (4–5½in) for skirts and trousers.
Very loose fit: Best described as oversized, this type of garment is very loosely fitted with ample room inside.

TRY IT

 125 *How can I get a good fit?*

Compare the finished-garment measurements printed on the pattern envelope or pattern tissue with your body measurements to see the difference in size and amount of ease allowed. Choose the most appropriate size to make up.

124

Understanding the pattern

Step-by-step instructions and diagrams are included inside the pattern envelope to inform of the best way to construct the garment. Information on selecting the most appropriate size and cutting layout advice are also given. Useful information is printed directly on the pattern tissue to help with accurate construction. These include symbols like arrows, notches and dots as well as notes to explain how many pieces need to be cut in fabric, interfacing and lining materials.

Construction symbols

Grain lines: These arrows are used to show the direction the paper pattern pieces should be placed on the grain of the weave, or sometimes they are used to indicate the direction of greatest stretch.
Curved arrow: A straight arrow which curves at each end to point to a solid line indicates that the pattern piece should be placed to a fold. This cuts a perfectly symmetrical shape.
Notches: These triangular marks on the cutting line are used to match panels accurately, for example, a sleeve into an armhole. It prevents confusion if there are similarly shaped pieces to be joined, like a panelled skirt. Single, double, and triple notches can be used to identify different parts on one garment.
Dots: Dots or large spots show the positions of darts, pockets and zips, and areas to be gathered or eased like a sleeve head.
Lines: Short lines are used to indicate button and buttonhole positions.
Arrow heads: These indicate the direction of sewing (often used for stay stitching) and the way material should be tucked or folded to form pleats.
Lengthening and shortening lines: These parallel pairs of lines show the best position to extend or reduce the pattern size to improve the fit. Simply cut the pattern and move apart to add length, or fold up the pattern for a shorter length.
Cutting lines: The solid line on the outside of a pattern is the cutting line.
Sewing lines: A dotted line is sometimes used to indicate the sewing line, although this is often not included as it is accepted that the sewing line lies 15mm (⅝in) inside the cutting line.

Multisize patterns

Many patterns today include several sizes printed together on the tissue pattern. This makes it easier to get a good fit as few people follow the exact standard size from which the patterns are graded. This makes it possible to make a well-fitting dress for someone who may have a size 12 hip with a size 8 waist and 10 bust.

The information given on a paper pattern helps with construction.

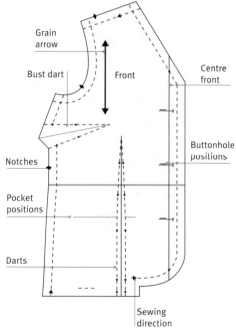

Fabric layouts

Each of the items included in the pack has a fabric-layout guide, usually two or three depending on the choice of fabric widths that can be used or whether the fabric is 'with nap' or not. The layout includes all the pattern pieces needed with an illustration of how to lay them on the fabric. It will also indicate whether to cut from single or double layers of fabric.

Joining fabrics

Whether your fabric is soft and light, heavy and stiff, or even stretchy, there is a perfect technique for joining every fabric together and neatening raw edges.

The simplest seam

A plain seam is the most common method of attaching two pieces of cloth together.

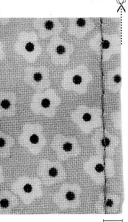

1 Place the fabric pieces face to face with the edges level and stitch parallel to the edge.

Seam allowance

2 The distance between the line of stitching and the raw edge is called the 'seam allowance' and, since many fabrics will fray or ravel, this raw edge should generally be neatened (see page 84). Iron the plain seam open for a flat finish.

French seam

In a French seam, all the raw edges are enclosed within the seam. Only two rows of stitching and a bit of trimming are required to complete it. Use on children's clothes, shirts, blouses, dresses and nightwear.

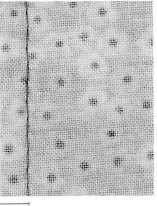

1 Place the wrong sides together with the edges matching. Sew with a standard straight stitch 6mm (¼in) from the edge. Trim the edges to 3mm (⅛in).

3mm (⅛in)

6mm (¼in)

2 Press open and fold the seam the opposite way so the right sides are now facing. Sew a line of stitching 6mm (¼in) from the edge.

FIX IT

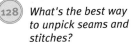

128 *What's the best way to unpick seams and stitches?*

No matter how experienced you are, sometimes things go wrong and you have to remove stitches or undo a seam. The easiest and least damaging way to unpick a seam is to cut every third stitch with a quick unpick or seam ripper on one side of the seam. Now turn it over and pull away the thread on the other side. This leaves tiny threads that can be picked off with fingers or sticky tape.

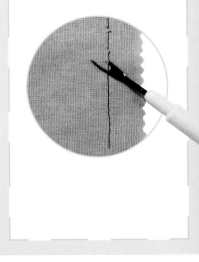

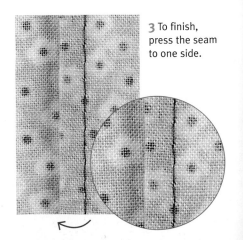

3 To finish, press the seam to one side.

129

Hairline seam

A hairline seam is similar to a French seam, but it is more delicate. Use on sheer, lightweight and translucent fabrics where a heavier seam would look ugly. As the seam allowances are tiny, this is not a strong seam and cannot withstand excessive strain.

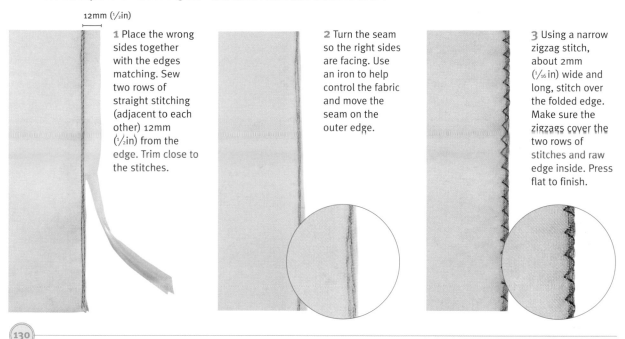

12mm (½in)

1 Place the wrong sides together with the edges matching. Sew two rows of straight stitching (adjacent to each other) 12mm (½in) from the edge. Trim close to the stitches.

2 Turn the seam so the right sides are facing. Use an iron to help control the fabric and move the seam on the outer edge.

3 Using a narrow zigzag stitch, about 2mm (¹⁄₁₆in) wide and long, stitch over the folded edge. Make sure the zigzags cover the two rows of stitches and raw edge inside. Press flat to finish.

130

Flat fell seam

The raw edges are tucked under and enclosed with topstitching in a flat fell seam, making the seam strong and hard-wearing. As it looks good from both sides, use for reversible garments and those that require a strong seam, like denim trousers, shirts, menswear and children's wear.

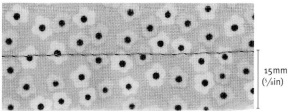

15mm (⅝in)

Fold over 3mm (⅛in) of upper seam allowance and press.

Cut lower seam allowance to 3mm (⅛in).

1 Place the wrong sides together, with the raw edges level. Sew a line of straight stitching 15mm (⅝in) parallel to the edge.

2 Press the seam allowance open. Trim one side to 3mm (⅛in) and fold over 3mm (⅛in) on the other side.

3 Fold the larger seam allowance over the smaller one and edge-stitch in place.

Fold upper seam down over lower and stitch in place.

131

Welt seam

Although a welt seam looks similar to a flat fell seam, it is less bulky and is only suitable for fabrics that don't fray. Suitable for coats and jackets made in boiled or felted wool.

  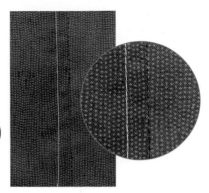

1 With right sides together and raw edges level, sew a plain seam 15mm (⅝in) from the edge.

2 Press the seam allowances to one side and trim the underlayer to 6mm (¼in).

3 Working from the right side, topstitch 6mm (¼in) from the seam through the fabric and the longer seam allowance below, trapping the trimmed allowance in between.

132

Mock flat fell seam

This simple-to-make seam has a similar appearance to a flat fell or welt seam from the right side; the only difference being that it is a lot quicker to sew. Use when time is limited as, for example, when shirt making.

  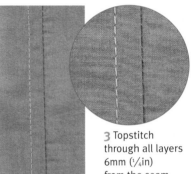

1 With right sides together and raw edges level, sew a plain seam 15mm (⅝in) from the edge.

2 Neaten the edges together with a zigzag stitch or serger. Press the seam allowances to one side and pin down from the right side.

3 Topstitch through all layers 6mm (¼in) from the seam.

6mm (¼in)

133

Lapped seam

A lapped seam has one fabric edge folded and placed on top of a lower flat edge to create a relatively flat seam. The two layers are edge-stitched and/or topstitched together. Often used for horizontal seams on garments and ideal for leather and suede, a row of topstitching added to the edge stitching makes it stronger.

1 Fold the seam allowance to the wrong side on the upper layer of cloth or, if the fabric does not fray, cut away the seam allowance entirely.

2 Place the upper folded or cut edge on top of the seam line of the lower fabric edge and pin together.

Folded upper fabric

Lower fabric

6mm (¼in)

3 Edge-stitch the seam to join. Add a parallel row of topstitching 6mm (¼in) away, if desired.

134

Quarter-inch seam

The quarter-inch seam is often used for projects where accuracy is important and small seam allowances are used, such as patchwork and constructing bras. Special sewing machine feet are available to help achieve a good result.

1 Fit a 6mm (¼in) foot to the sewing machine or (if possible) move the needle position 6mm (¼in) from the edge of the standard foot. With right sides facing, place the raw edge of the fabrics to be joined, to the edge of the sewing machine foot.

2 Sew a line of straight stitching. Press both seam allowances to one side.

Press both seam allowances to one side.

3 For garments, press horizontal seams downwards and for patchwork projects, press in the direction of the darker shade of fabric.

135

Smooth seams

To achieve a perfectly smooth, wrinkle-free seam on all types of fabric, follow these three steps.

1 Iron the stitches of the seam flat.

2 Press the seam open with the point of the iron over the centre of the seam and not the seam allowances (this causes ridges to be seen on the right side).

3 Turn over and iron lightly over the surface of the fabric and seam. (Use a pressing cloth for this last stage if the fabric is delicate.)

(136)

Nine
NEATENERS

Most woven and knitted fabrics tend to fray or ravel, so cut edges need to be finished to prevent them from coming apart. Match your method to the type of fabric construction (loosely woven, stiff or knitted), the weight of the fabric and where it is to be used (a reversible jacket or a child's dress, for example).

1 Pinking shears

Pinking shears have blades that produce a zigzag or notched edge. This helps limit the ravelling of the fabric threads.

2 Zigzag stitch

Set the sewing machine to width 10spi (2mm), length 12spi (1.5mm), and sew ¹⁄₈in (3mm) parallel to the edge. Carefully trim the excess fabric away to leave a smooth edge. Press to finish.

3 Sewing machine serging

Sew right on the raw edge – if a preprogrammed overcasting stitch and a suitable serging foot are available for your model of machine. Select the stitch and place the foot guide to the neatly cut raw edge. Stitch along the length of the edge.

4 Serging

For a quick, neat, professional finish, thread up both lower loopers and one needle (left for a wide stitch coverage and right for a narrower finish). Serge the seam edge, removing 1mm (¹⁄₁₆in) of the fabric with the blade. Press flat for a perfect finish.

5 Straight stitch

Tuck 3mm (¹⁄₈in) of the raw edge to the wrong side and sew in place with a straight stitch. Use an iron to press the tuck first. Although a more bulky method, this is a quick technique when a straight stitch machine is all that is available.

6 Taped edge

Sew a narrow cotton tape or ribbon over the fabric edge for a neat finish that will help prevent ravelling raw edges.

7 Hong Kong finish

This high-class method of neatening a raw edge is a real luxury. Cut a 32mm (1¹⁄₄in) bias strip and sew to the right side of the fabric, 6mm (¹⁄₄in) from the edge. Trim to 3mm (¹⁄₈in), then wrap the bias strip round the edge, and stitch in the ditch to hold it in place. Trim away excess fabric and press for a flat finish.

8 Bound edge

A bound edge is similar to a Hong Kong finish but with more bulk. Place the edge of the bias tape (bought or self-made) to the raw edge and sew a 6mm (¹⁄₄in) seam. Wrap the bias tape over the edge, tucking in the cut edge for a neat finish on both sides. Hold the layers together with hand-sewn hemming stitches or a line of straight machining.

9 Overcasting

This hand-sewn finish is simple to do but rarely found today. Thread up a needle and wrap horizontal stitches over the raw edge.

① ② ③ ④ ⑤ ⑥ ⑦ ⑧

MAKE IT!

(137) Recycled shopping bag

This is a great way of recycling an old sheet or curtain. Follow these seven simple steps.

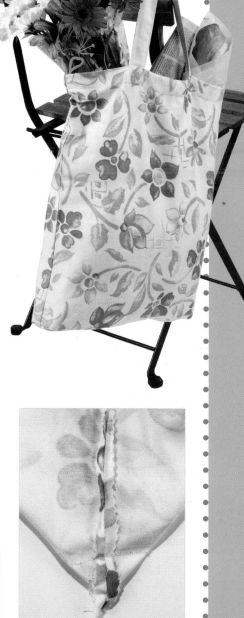

1 Cut two rectangles of cloth approximately 46 x 51cm (18 x 20in) for the front and back and two 46 x 10cm (18 x 4in) for the straps.

2 Place the right sides of the bag together. Sew three sides with a 15mm (⅝in) seam. Neaten the edges. Press flat and turn through.

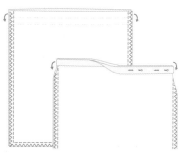

3 Make a double hem on the open upper edge by folding down 2.5cm (1in) twice. Pin the hem in place and set aside.

4 Make the straps by folding each in half lengthwise and tucking the raw edges to the centre fold on the wrong side. Refold and topstitch on both sides to secure.

5 Position the handles centrally. Tuck the ends of the straps under the hem and catch in place when the hem is stitched down.

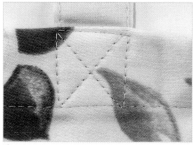

6 Stitch crosses to reinforce the handle straps.

7 Give the bag depth by folding the bottom corners so the seams lie on top of each other. Sew across at 45 degrees.

3-D shaping

Fabric is flat and two-dimensional but by clever cutting, and with different construction techniques like the ones detailed below, you can create endless shapes to suit numerous figure variations.

(138) Gathering

This involves reducing the length of one piece of fabric to fit another by making gathers or tiny pleats. Use on a sleeve head to join a sleeve to a shoulder, on the waist of a child's skirt, or to create a full frill around a cushion or pillow.

1 Set the sewing machine to straight stitch with the longest stitch available.

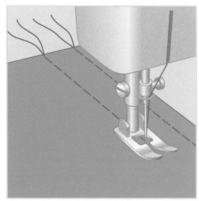

2 With right side uppermost, sew two parallel rows of stitching 6mm (¼in) apart. Leave thread tails of 7.5cm (3in) at either end.

3 Pull up the fabric to the required length while creating even gathers along the length. When the right length is achieved, place a pin at each end and wrap the tails around the pins.

(139) Gathering long or heavy fabrics

• To gather a long piece of fabric, divide the length into manageable sections to prevent the thread from breaking.
• For heavier weights of fabric, sew a zigzag stitch over a length of cord to encase it.

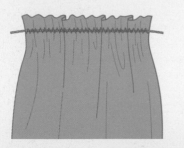

4 Pin the gathered length to the band, yoke, or cuff. Set the sewing machine to a standard stitch length – about 10spi (2.5mm) – and sew the seam.

5 Carefully pull out all the basting and gathering threads. Press into the fullness to finish.

Place pins at either end of the two rows of easing stitches.
Tie off the threads to hold the easing in place for stitching.

140

Easing

Easing occurs where one piece of fabric is reduced slightly in length to fit another by making tiny, invisible pleats. Use on a sleeve head (as shown below) to join a sleeve to a shoulder on a jacket or blouse, or on the waist of a straight or A-line skirt.

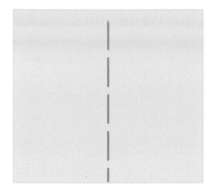

1 Set the sewing machine to the longest straight stitch.

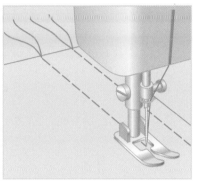

2 With right side uppermost, sew two parallel rows of straight stitch on either side of the seam line 3mm (⅛in) apart. Do not cut the thread tails off. Working from the wrong side of the fabric, place a pin across the stitches at one end and wrap the tails around it.

3 Pull up the fabric along the gathering threads to ease it to the size of the adjoining fabric, without any tucks or gathers. Place a pin at the other and wrap the other tails around it to secure the easing.

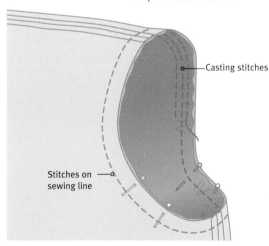

Casting stitches

Stitches on sewing line

4 Place the eased fabric to the flat piece with right sides together. Pin along the seam line (in between the two rows of easing). Set the sewing machine to a standard stitch length – about 10spi (2.5mm) – and sew the seam, making sure no tucks appear in the eased fabric.

5 Remove all the gathering threads by carefully pulling them out. Press to create a smooth finish.

The finished eased sleeve

An eased sleeve head is smooth with no tucks or gathers.

MAKE IT!

Frilly apron

Choose a bright print to match the kitchen decor in a fabric that is easily laundered, and add a pretty frill.

1 Make a pattern from newspaper. Check the size is suitable for the wearer, fold in half and trim to ensure it is symmetrical.

2 Measure the curved edge. Cut a strip of fabric double this length by 10cm (4in) wide.

3 Cut a length of fabric for the waistband and ties. This should be 10cm (4in) wide by 150–200cm (60–80in) long.

4 Fold the strip of fabric for the frill in half with the wrong sides together. Divide the length into four even portions. Sew two rows of machine gathers (see page 86) through both layers next to the raw edges.

5 Pull up the gathers from the underside and arrange the fullness evenly along the length.

6 Place the frill to the apron with right sides together and the three raw edges level. Pin and machine together in between the rows of gathering stitches. Remove the gathering stitches.

7 Neaten the raw edges of the frilled edge with a serger or zigzag stitch (see page 84). Gather the top edge of the apron as for the frill and arrange fullness evenly.

8 Fold the waistband and ties in half, with wrong sides on the inside. Tuck in a 15mm (⅝in) seam allowance on all sides.

9 Open the band and place the centre to the centre of the apron's top edge with right sides facing. Pin and sew together along the top edge of the apron.

10 Refold the band and edge-stitch together to enclose all the raw edges. Secure the inside of the band to the apron.

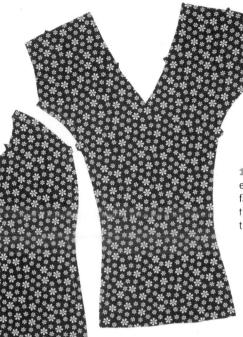

142

Shaped or princess seams

These long, vertical, curving seams extend from the armhole or shoulder to the hem of a fitted dress. They require careful snipping and notching on the wrong side for a perfectly smooth result. Use on close-fitting dresses to give shape over the bust, waist and hip.

1 Stay-stitch the curved edges of each piece of fabric 3mm (⅛in) from the sewing line within the seam allowance.

2 Snip into the seam allowance up to the stay stitching on the concave parts of the seam.

FIX IT

143 *How do I stop my seams from stretching?*

Shoulder seams, princess seams and neckline edges do not follow the straight grain of the fabric. To avoid them stretching and distorting when sewing, prepare each layer before joining by sewing a line of straight stitching – about 8spi (3mm) in length – close to the seam line within the seam allowance. This stabilizes the fabric edge ready for sewing.

3 With right sides facing, place the fabric edges together, matching up the seam lines and any notches or balance points.

4 Pin and/or baste the seam 15mm (⅝in) from the edge and smooth out any wrinkles. (The snipped edges should make this easier.)

5 Machine along the seam line with a straight stitch and then remove the basting thread.

144

Darts

Darts are pinched triangles of fabric sewn to add shaping to a garment. Use at the waist of a skirt or trousers or on the bodice of a blouse or dress. Instructions will normally be included on a commercial paper pattern.

1 With right sides together, fold the fabric through the centre of the dart, matching any pattern markings. Draw a curved sewing line on the fabric to give a smooth finish rather than an abrupt point.

2 Pin and/or baste together. Starting from the wider end and using a standard-length straight stitch, sew on the sewing line towards the point.

3 At the point, take two stitches on the fold of the fabric and raise the needle. Thread the tails onto a 'hand-sewing' needle and finish off before cutting them.

4 Iron the dart using the three-step method on page 83. Use a tailor's ham under the dart to help with shaping.

145

Double-ended darts

When sewing a double-ended dart, sew from the middle to the point overlapping the stitches to secure the ends.

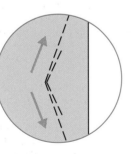

146

Pressing tips for darts

Follow these three key pointers for easy pressing for darts.

Press horizontal darts downwards.

Press vertical darts either to the centre or the side seams but be consistent.

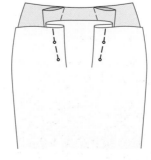

Do not sew darts in linings at the waist of a skirt or trousers, just form a tuck to take up the excess fabric.

Desirable draping

When woven fabric is cut on the bias (or cross grain), it gains a softer draping quality because it is not constrained by the grain. As the woven threads are pulled diagonally, the fabric stretches slightly and this movement gives a softer appearance. As a result, bias-cut skirt and dress panels hang more gracefully than those cut with the grain.

To cut on the bias is to cut diagonally across the woven threads of a fabric: it gives a softer drape, as in this skirt.

147 Cutting on the bias

• Cover the work surface with a smooth cotton sheet. Lay down your fabric in a single layer. The sheet prevents the fabric from shifting or distorting when the pattern pieces are pinned on and cut out.

• Cut the pattern pieces from a single layer of fabric to ensure perfectly symmetrical panels.

• Cut with sharp, long-bladed scissors to get a smooth edge.

• If the fabric pieces are small enough, use a rotary cutter and mat. This method is ideal when making silk camisoles and French panties.

• Use a 2.5cm (1in) seam allowance when cutting fabric panels on the bias, as the standard 15mm (⅝in) may be reduced as the fabric is pulled and stretched. The fabric is a little more stable and easier to work with 2.5cm (1in) from the edge.

Find the true bias with a diagonal fold.

Place each pattern piece on the true bias, not the grain.

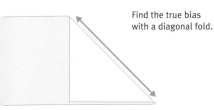

Woven fabric will stretch when pulled across the grain.

148 Sewing on the bias

Once you have followed the advice for cutting out, there are a few more things to consider when handling and sewing garments with panels cut on the bias. To achieve the best finish possible try these suggestions.

Walking foot

Attach a walking foot to the sewing machine and use a stretch stitch or narrow zigzag stitch (see page 84). The finished seam tends not to ripple but the stretch stitch will accommodate any movement that might occur when the seam is left to hang.

Pulling fabric

When machine sewing a seam, pull the fabric gently with your hands placed in front of and behind the needle. This puts extra stitches into the seam to cope with any stretching that might take place as the fabric is left to hang. The resulting seam may appear rippled but this can normally be ironed out.

FIX IT

149 Wondering why your bias-cut garments are drooping and stretching?

The stability of the fabric is lost when you sew garments off the grain. It is sometimes difficult to cut accurately shaped panels, so the left and right sides of a dress, for instance, may not drape symmetrically. Here's why:

• The hem may be uneven, with unintentional, asymmetric seams!

• The asymmetric draping puts stress on the seams, stretching them and even causing the threads to break.

• Bias-cut garments may appear too big, even though the correct size was chosen.

• Seam allowances can effectively shrink because, when they are pulled, they become longer but narrower.

Don't be put off when sewing bias styles; there are specific techniques shown here that can be adopted to overcome these problems and that will allow you to achieve great results.

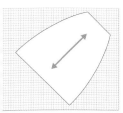

Pleats

Pleats are folds of fabric normally trapped at one end and loose at the other, and can be partially stitched down into position. They come in various formations and are sometimes crisp and sharp but they can be soft and draping too. Pleats are used to control the fullness of fabric and to add style. The way they are folded determines their type.

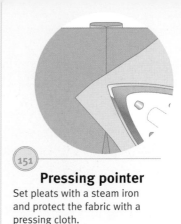

151

Pressing pointer
Set pleats with a steam iron and protect the fabric with a pressing cloth.

150

Knife pleats

Knife pleats are folds of fabric that all lie in the same direction (as, for example, in a Scottish kilt). They may be used in small numbers or for an entire part of a garment. They may be sharply creased or gently folded, depending on the style required, and may be stitched down or hang free.

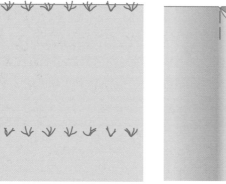

1 Mark the size and position of the pleats accurately with tailor's tacks or chalk.

2 Baste at least the top 5cm (2in) of the pleats or the entire length of the pleat for a more accurate finish. Press the pleats (in one direction) to form sharp creases in the folds. Edge-stitch each pleat to hip level or leave them loose if preferred. Attach a yoke or waistband as necessary.

Knife pleats can be stitched down or left free (as above).

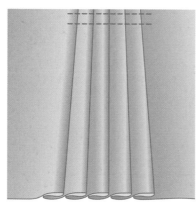

3 When stitched in place, remove all basting stitches and press the garment.

A traditional kilt features knife pleats.

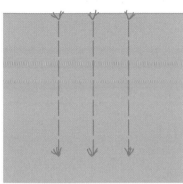

152

Inverted pleats

An inverted pleat consists of two folds that face each other. Like a knife pleat, it can be stitched down or left to hang free from a seam or waistband, and may be either soft or pressed crisply.

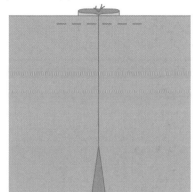

1 Mark the position and size of the pleat with tailor's tacks or chalk (on the wrong side of the fabric).

2 Fold the pleat through the centre with the right sides of the fabric facing. Machine sew a straight stitch along the marked line. Baste from here to the hem.

3 Press the line of stitching and fold so the centre crease lies directly below the seam. Baste within the seam allowance. Press the inverted pleat and remove basting stitches.

153

Box pleats

A box pleat is a reversed inverted pleat. The two folds face away from each other on the surface giving a wide vertical pleat. Use box pleats on skirts, pockets and the centre back of a shirt where it meets the yoke.

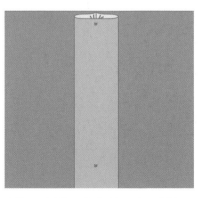

1 Mark the position and size of the pleat with tailor's tacks or chalk (on the wrong side of the fabric).

2 Fold the pleat through the centre with the wrong sides of the fabric facing. Machine sew a straight stitch along the marked line. Baste from the base of the stitching to the hem.

3 Press the line of stitching, then fold so the centre seam lies flat and directly below the centre of the box pleat. Baste within the seam allowance. Press the box pleat using a cloth to protect the surface and remove the basting stitches.

Hemming

Choosing the right hem for each project is essential. Some garment styles and fabrics need a narrow hem, while others require a heavier, deeper edge. A serged rolled hem is ideal for a circular skirt made in a fine silk cloth, while a deep single-folded hem, neatened with a Hong Kong finish, is better for a woollen winter coat.

154

Hand versus machine

The choice is yours but for strength choose a machined hem and for an invisible finish choose a hand-sewn stitch. If you wish to emulate a bought garment use a machined topstitched hem; if you want your garments to look like couture originals, use a hand-stitched hem.

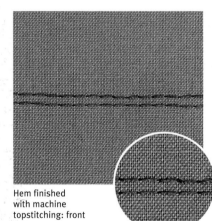

Hem finished with machine topstitching: front

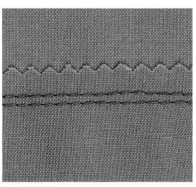

Hem finished with machine topstitching: back

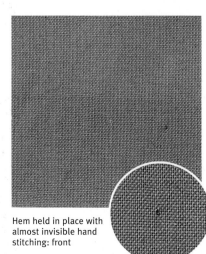

Hem held in place with almost invisible hand stitching: front

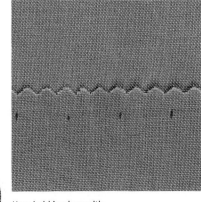

Hem held in place with almost invisible hand stitching: back

155

Four

STEPS TO A PERFECT HEM

1 **Get a friend to help:** If you can't find one, buy a dress form (tailor's dummy) and set it to your own size and height.

2 **Wear the shoes** you're going to accessorize the garment with.

3 **Use a long ruler** or a yard (metre) stick and measure the level from the floor to the chosen hem length with chalk or pins.

4 **Trim at a suitable length** below the chalk line to give the hem the space to turn up. Finish as required. Too much excess fabric can give a bulky finish.

156

Single-folded hem

Follow the simple steps below for folding single-folded hems of coats, skirts, trousers, and many other garments.

1 Neaten the raw edge with a method to suit the fabric weight (see page 84 for suggestions).

2 Fold up the wrong side to the correct length. Pin, press and baste if necessary.

3 Sew the hem in place with topstitching, or by hand with a lock stitch or slip hemming.

4 Remove basting and iron lightly over the hem edge. Use a pressing cloth if necessary.

157 Double-folded hem

The raw edges are completely concealed on a double-folded hem because the hem folds up over itself to hide the edge in the hem fold. Use on curtains with a 10cm (4in) hem to give weight and help curtains to hang well. Use a narrower hem on trousers and denim, and a very narrow one on the lower edge of a shirt.

Double-folded top-stitched hem (front)

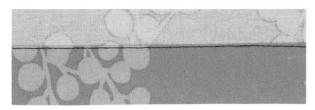

Double-folded top-stitched hem (back)

Mark the level of the hem required on the wrong side of the fabric. Fold the raw edge to this line. Fold the hem up once more to hide the edge inside. Press, pin and, if necessary, baste in position. Topstitch close to the upper edge, sewing from the right side. Remove basting thread and press to finish.

Note:
A topstitch thread is thicker and will give a more prominent finish to the stitch. The appearance of the hem is also improved if the stitch length is increased to 8spi (3mm) long.

FIX IT

159 *Can't find a topstitch thread in a suitable colour?*

If you cannot find a topstitch thread in a suitable colour, use two ordinary threads. Feed them both through the sewing machine guides and needle together then stitch as normal. You may need an embroidery needle or topstitch needle to accommodate the two threads.

158 Faced hem

On a curved or shaped hem, a facing is the best way to produce a neat, flat finish. It is a separate piece of fabric cut to the same shape as the hem and sewn to the hem edge. Use to finish the hem on a full wedding dress or on a scalloped edge.

1 Using a paper pattern, trace off a facing of the lower 7.5cm (3in) of the pattern pieces to be hemmed.

2 Cut the facings in the same fabric as the garment. (On a thick fabric, such as fur, a lighter-weight facing could be used to reduce bulk.)

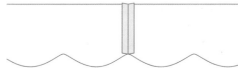

3 Join the facing pieces together and press the seams open.

4 Place the facing to the garment hem with right sides together and the seams matching. Pin and then sew together.

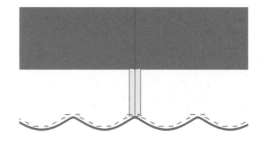

5 Trim the raw edges to 6mm (¼in). Fold up into place with the seam slightly towards the wrong side so it is out of sight. Press the edge for a flat finish.

6 Tuck under or neaten the facing edge and finish the hem with a lock stitch or slip stitch (page 59).

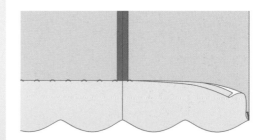

160

Machine blind hem

When you have mastered the appropriate folding and manipulation, this is a quick and easy hem suitable for some, but not all, projects. The machine stitches mostly on the hem on the inside and catches regular stitches through the fabric to hold it in position. The machine blind hem is ideal for curtains or for trousers and works best on thicker fabrics where the stitches are not visible from the right side.

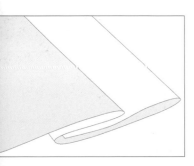

1 Fold up the hem. Pin in the middle. Fold the hem back on itself, leaving it flat

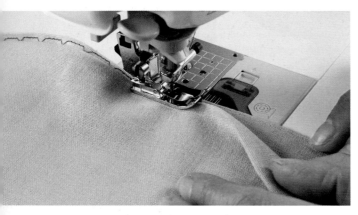

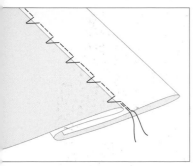

2 Fit a blind hem foot to the sewing machine and set to a blind hem stitch (check the manual).

3 Place the hem under the foot with the folded edge against the guide. Sew through the hem, catching the fold when the needle swings to the left.

4 Adjust the hem and press flat.

Regular stitches are seen on the front where the thread catches the fabric.

161

Glued hem

Some difficult-to-sew fabrics can be glued in place rather than sewn. You can use a rubber solution, PVA glue or a fusible web which, when heated with an iron, will secure two layers of fabric together. Use on waterproof fabric, leather or animal fur, or as a quick fix when there is no time to hem conventionally.

Iron the hem but not the edge stitching as this may cause a ridge to be seen from the right side.

1 Spread glue on the wrong side of the hem edge and fold up into place.

2 Hold the hem in place with weights or clothes pins until the glue is dry.

Alternatively:

1 Place a strip of heat-fusible web along the hem edge (on the wrong side of the fabric) and fold up into position. Secure with pins.

2 Iron over the hem carefully to heat and fuse the layers together. Remove the pins while you work. Leave to cool. Not all glues or iron-on strips are washable. Check manufacturer's details first to avoid disappointment!

162

Pressing points for hems

Avoiding ridges
On the inside, slip the iron under the flap of the hem to prevent an obvious ridge from being created on the right side.

Avoid those pins!
Don't press over pins. This may mark or damage the fabric and pins with large heads may melt!

Making a rolled hem

There are three main methods: sewing machine, hand and serger. The choice is normally dictated by the equipment available. Use on chiffon, habotai silk and other fine, lightweight fabrics. A full, floaty skirt or a printed chiffon scarf will look beautiful with a narrow, delicate rolled hem. Use a serger for medium to lightweight skirts, dresses and T-shirts, and on silk or chiffon scarves. When the fabric is pulled during the sewing process it produces a lettuce edge. Use on stretch fabrics, bias-cut edges on evening wear, or little girls' clothing for a pretty finish.

A serged rolled hem gives a delicate finish on lightweight and sheer fabrics.

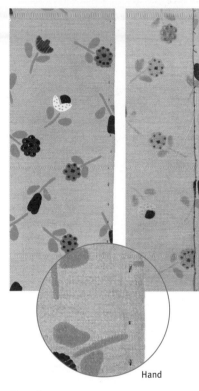

Hand

Sewing machine

Hand

1 Roll the edge to the wrong side, concealing the raw edge inside.

2 Make small slip stitches to hold the hem in place.

Sewing machine

1 Fit a rolled hem foot to the sewing machine. These feet have a curved plate to feed the fabric under the needle in a narrow fold. They vary in width, depending on the depth of finish required.

2 Set the machine to a straight stitch or choose a zigzag just wide enough to cover the rolled edge.

3 Fold a small length of the hem over twice towards the wrong side of the fabric. Place this under the needle and lower the needle to hold it in place.

4 Uncurl the fold in front of the needle and slip this through the curve in the rolled hem foot. Lower the presser foot and sew steadily, continuing to feed the fabric edge into the foot and trapping the folded hem with the stitches as you sew.

5 If the hem is continuous, slip the fabric out of the foot for the last 5cm (2in) and manipulate by hand before completing the last of the stitches. This produces a neater join.

Using a serger to create hems

1 Follow the instruction manual to set the serger to rolled hemming.

2 Mark the hem length with chalk on the right side of the fabric.

3 Feed the fabric edge under the presser foot with the chalked line to the blade. This will cut off the excess and form the rolled hem over the raw fabric edge.

A serged rolled hem completely encases the fabric edge with threads.

FIX IT

(165) *How do I create an invisible hem on a silk skirt?*

Underline (see page 109) the entire skirt with tulle or silk organza to provide a skeleton. Fold up the hem and pin in place. Hand sew in position, catching only the underlining (not the outer fabric) to the hem. No stitches will be visible on the right side of the garment.

FIX IT

(166) *How do I shorten a T-shirt?*

T-shirt fabric stretches, which can lead to broken threads or wavy hems. The best way to shorten a T-shirt is to trim to 12mm (½in) below the required length and neaten this raw edge with a serger or a zigzag stitch. Fold up to the wrong side and pin or baste in place. Sew the hem in position with a twin needle using colour-matching thread and a walking foot attached to the machine. No one will ever know you've made an alteration!

---

(167)

Lettuce edge

Create a lettuce hem on a stretch knit fabric or a bias-cut woven fabric by pulling on the cloth as the edge is serged. The result is a pretty, curly edge. What is actually happening is that extra stitches are being forced into the hem so the edge is permanently stretched to produce this wavy finish. Lovely for little girls' and ladies' wear.

Cut a narrow bias strip and finish each edge with lettuce hemming. Sew this on to a jacket edge for an attractive textured finish.

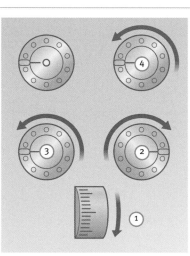

1 Set the serger for rolled hemming by removing the left needle, shortening the stitch length (1), tightening the lower looper tension (2), and loosening the upper looper tension (3). You can also loosen the needle thread tension (4). For best results consult the serger manual.

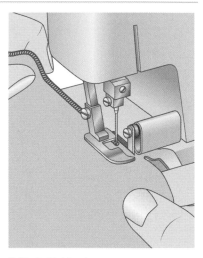

2 Start stitching to secure the needle in the fabric. Gently pull the fabric in front of the needle while continuing to sew. When the hem is completed, stretch the hem to emphasize the wavy effect.

Hemming stretch fabric

Fabric with knitted construction is stretchy, which makes it ideal for comfortable, easy-to-fit garments but can be difficult to hem neatly. The hem of a stretch fabric may ripple when sewn, or the threads may break as the material is pulled, but the stitches don't! However, there are solutions.

Twin needle

Using a twin needle can create a manufactured appearance. Fit a twin needle and select a straight stitch to hold up a hem. The single bobbin thread below acts like a zigzag and allows the hem to stretch with the fabric and hence does not break.

Walking foot

Choose a suitable stitch and attach a walking foot to the sewing machine. The foot walks over the fabric and does not allow it to stretch in the way that a standard foot does. This prevents the rippling that sometimes occurs and which can't always be pressed out later with an iron.

Stretch stitch

Triple stitch

Narrow zigzag stitch

Triple or zigzag stitch

Choose a machine stretch stitch. Both triple stitch (three stitches forwards and one back) and narrow zigzag stitch add stretch to a line of stitching. This means that the stitches of a hem will move when a garment is pulled on or off.

Decorative stitch

Choose a decorative stitch. The varying angles of the stitches will allow the hem to move when the fabric is stretched so the threads will not break.

Four-thread serging

Use a serger as the differential feed, combined with the formation of the stitch, works well on stretchy fabric, preventing rippling and broken threads.

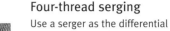

Four-thread serging gives a secure seam.

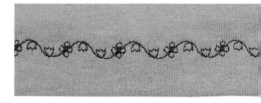

Add a hem band

Finish a hem with a folded band for a quick finish on stretch fabric.

1 Cut a strip of the same fabric in the direction of greatest stretch and fold it in half.

2 Cut the folded strip 20 per cent less than the length of the hem and stretch the band to fit the hem.

3 Place the folded band to the edge. Stitch in place and neaten the edge.

4 Press the band down and raw edges up to finish.

FIX IT

170 *What sort of needle should I use?*

For best results when hemming with stretch knits, choose a stretch, jersey or ballpoint needle. The rounded end slips between the threads forming perfect stitches. Stretch twin needles are also available.

Best ways with edges

Hems are not the only vertical edges that need to be neatened and finished; there are also cuffs and necklines. Facings, bindings, bands and lace can be used for an edge. Follow these suggestions and you'll never hear a friend ask: 'Did you make that yourself?'

171

The easiest edge finish ever

If you are looking for a quick method to neaten an edge on a front band or cuff, this is the one you need. It is ideal for a wrapped robe in polyester or silk satin and also for stretch cotton garments like T-shirts or cardigans (see page 99).

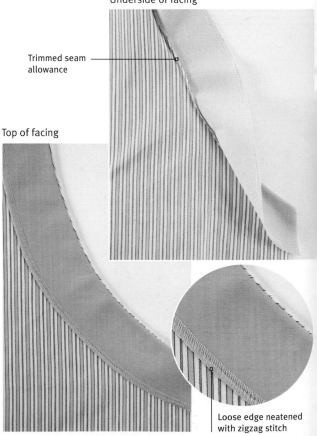

1 Cut a band twice the width by the required length and add seam allowances. (Join these strips with plain seams if necessary – at the back neck of a robe, for example.) Fold the band in half lengthwise, with the wrong sides to the inside.

2 Pin the band to the right side of the garment edge. Sew a 15mm (⅝in) seam. Tuck in the hem edge at the bottom.

3 Trim and neaten the raw edge. Fold the band to the front with the neatened edge to the inside and press flat. Slip-stitch the tucked-in hem edge of the band.

172

Making a facing

A piece of fabric sewn and ironed to the wrong side to neaten and support an edge gives a smooth finish that is especially useful for a shaped edge. Use on the armholes, neckline and front edge of a sleeveless dress. Be warned: a facing can slip to the right side of a garment if not sewn down securely.

1 Neaten the loose edge of the facing with a zigzag stitch or serger (see page 84).

2 Place the facing to the garment edge with right sides together and pin.

3 Machine sew on the seam line. Trim away (and snip if necessary) any excess seam allowance.

4 Take the facing to the wrong side and press in place with the seam slightly towards the wrong side.

Underside of facing

Trimmed seam allowance

Top of facing

Loose edge neatened with zigzag stitch

FIX IT

173 *How do I keep a facing in place?*

A sleeveless top is often finished with armhole facings but these can move from the inside to the outside during wear. To keep them in place, wind fusible thread onto a bobbin by hand and understitch the raw edges to the facing. Sew from the facing side. When finished, press the facing down into place with an iron. The fusible thread will 'glue' the facings to the inside of the bodice and they should not work their way out when worn.

174

Lace edge

Lace edging gives a delicate finish with little bulk. It is lapped over the fabric and the fabric is then cut away underneath, leaving a shaped lace edge. Ideal for lingerie and nightwear, a lace edge can also be pretty on ladies' and children's clothing. Lace cannot be used on fabrics that fray badly, where a different method of finishing is required.

1 Lap the lace over the garment edge with both fabric and lace facing up. Pin the layers together. Set the sewing machine to a zigzag about 12spi (2mm) long and 12spi (2mm) wide.

2 Zigzag over the inside edge of the lace through both layers, removing the pins in the process. Trim away the excess fabric of the seam allowance up to the zigzag stitching, leaving the lace above it.

MAKE IT!

175 **Cotton napkin**

You can cut napkins and tablecloth to size by removing seam allowances. Buy pre-folded bias binding and fold it in half lengthways. Pin it over the outside edge of the napkins and tablecloth, mitring the corners. Fit a wing needle to the sewing machine and sew with a blanket-style stitch. The wing needle makes small holes in the tablecloth and the blanket stitch secures the binding to the edge, giving a decorative hem.

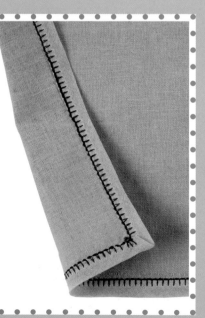

176 Quick and easy pennants

Make quick and easy pennants for your summer fair or party. Cut lots of triangles of brightly coloured fabric and join them with folded bias binding.

177 Purchased bias tape

Bias tape can be purchased as regular double-fold bias tape or foldover braid. Either can be used to encase raw edges, and the choice will depend on the finished project. For a child's garment, contrasting colourful binding looks good, whereas for an edge-to-edge jacket, decorative foldover braid would be more suitable. When buying the tape, check that it requires the same laundry care as the main fabric.

178 Bias binding

A fabric band cut on the bias, folded and sewn over a raw edge will completely enclose the raw edges and give a neat, firm edge. Use on the front, neck and hem of an edge-to-edge Chanel-style jacket, a tablecloth or an apron. Bias binding produces a thick finish because there are four layers of fabric covering the edge, so it is not suitable for all fabrics.

1 Iron the bias binding in half lengthwise. Place the folded binding over the raw edge of your project and pin in place.

2 Edge-stitch through all layers. Close the binding edge catching the binding on the lower side at the same time. This will secure the binding to the fabric edge.

Bias binding lies flat around a curve, leaving no tucks or wrinkles.

Use bias binding to neaten the neck edge of a collarless jacket.

Luxury linings

A lining improves so many things: curtains hang better; jackets slide on and off smoothly; skirts last longer; and the contents of a purse are much more secure. In addition, a lining conceals all the raw edges, giving a much-improved finish.

179

Types of lining

A lining is made to neaten the inside, add body or weight, or sometimes stabilize an outer fabric. It is generally made as a separate piece and dropped in, with all the raw edges facing each other, before being secured.

Habotai silk

Light and soft, this natural fibre is warm to the touch. Perfect for a fine wool blazer or jacket.

Fleece

Good for warmth, but fleece tends to cling, so it is not always suitable. Use for sleeping bags, hats and short, casual winter jackets as a warm lining for a waterproof outer layer.

Curtain lining

Available in neutral shades, curtain lining often has a satin weave with a low shine. Curtains are lined to add body, prevent fading and lengthen life.

Blackout lining

Blackout lining is used for curtains to keep out the light. However, unless they are long and fitted at a large window, this lining will not allow the curtains to drape naturally as it is very stiff.

Dress lining (rayon or polyester)

Dress lining is suitable for most projects and available in many colours. Take care with the iron as dress lining melts easily!

Satin lining

Satin has a shiny surface that looks luxurious and gives a lovely finish to a garment or bag. The surface threads, which give the shine, are easily damaged, so perhaps keep it for special occasion wear.

Novelty

For a fun lining on a child's garment, choose a printed fabric with cars, trucks, stripes, fairies or flowers.

180

Choosing the right lining

It is important to think carefully about the lining of a garment and to make an appropriate choice. Here are a few considerations.

Washing

For a jacket requiring dry cleaning, a luxurious silk might be ideal, but for a machine-washable dress or skirt, the lining will need similar treatment, so a polyester or rayon would be more appropriate.

Anti-static

Choose a lining with an anti-static finish which will not cling to the body when worn. This is more important with looser styles of dresses and skirts where the lining gets trapped around the knees and works its way up.

Satin weave

A lining with a smooth surface in a satin weave will allow clothing to slide on and off with ease and be very comfortable to wear. It also catches the light and looks expensive.

Warmth

When keeping warm is a requirement, think carefully about the lining. A short jacket with a fleece or fur lining may be fine but in the case of a long coat, clothing beneath it may ride up depending on the direction of the pile.

Size

When cutting the lining of a bodice or jacket, cut the armhole slightly smaller to fit closer to the body and to give a smoother finish.

Pattern

When making clothes, a pattern for a lining is not always included. This is not a problem: you can add one if you wish. See pages 106–108 for suggestions.

Curtains

When selecting a curtain lining, consider whether light reduction is the primary factor. The curtain fabric may already be dark enough in colour or may have a weave thick enough to reduce some of the light, so a standard curtain lining may be sufficient. Other drapes may need a denser lining fabric or blackout lining to achieve a dark room.

(181)

How to reline a handbag

A lining is made to cover the inside of a bag to neaten it, add body or weight, or sometimes stabilize an outer fabric. It is generally made as a separate piece and dropped in, with all the raw edges facing each other, before being stitched by hand.

Take care not to remove the construction stitches of the bag.

2 Make a pattern or template using the removed lining, or follow the outline of the bag itself to achieve the right shape and size.

1 Remove the existing lining, if there is one, by unpicking the stitches.

3 Using the template, cut out two pieces of lining fabric and two pieces of fusible interfacing.

4 Fuse the interfacing to the wrong side of the lining fabric with a hot iron. Use a pressing cloth to protect the fabric and interfacing from the hot iron. Press a 1cm (½in) hem along the top edges. Pin the right sides of the lining together

5 Sew with a 1cm (½in) seam allowance. Don't forget to secure the thread ends for added strength.

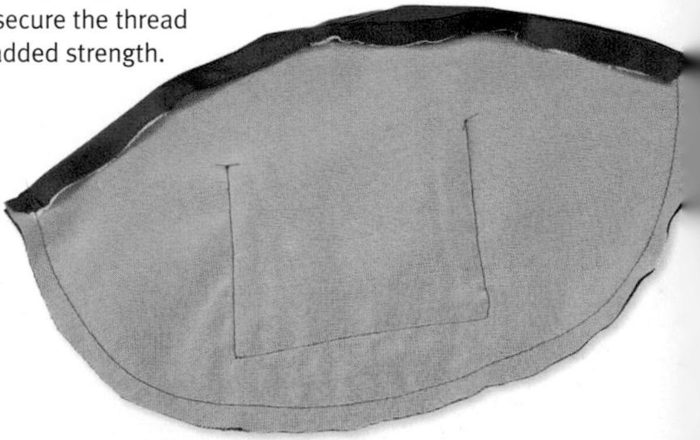

TRY IT

(182) *Inside pocket*

Add a useful pocket (see page 115) to the inside of the lining. Simply stitch onto the right side at the end of step 3, shown above.

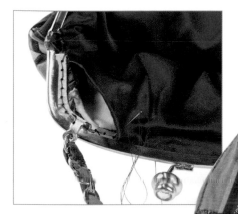

6 Drop the lining into the bag and sew in place. Use a double thread and use any existing stitch holes, or sew carefully to the cloth on the inside of the bag. Make sure the lining is secure and the stitches are not visible on the right side.

FIX IT

183 *How do I mend a hole in the lining of a bag?*

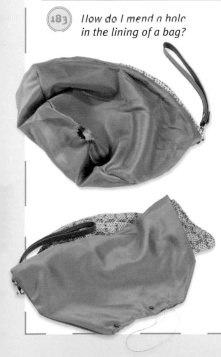

1 Check the damage. If the threads are worn near the seam it may be possible to shorten the lining and make a new seam.

2 Pull out the lining, refold and restitch across the new seam line from the right side. Do this by hand with a slip stitch through the folds across the length of the seam.

Alternatively, using fabric of a similar colour and type, make a patch slightly bigger than the hole and press under the edges. Place over the hole and hand sew with tiny stitches to secure it in place.

(184)

Lining a jacket

Adding a lining to a jacket – shop-bought or home-made – isn't difficult. All you require is pattern paper (or newspaper), some suitable lining fabric and your sewing kit.

1 Lay a large piece of paper on a flat working area. Turn the jacket inside out and tuck the sleeves inside. Adjust the side and armhole seams so they are outermost. Place the jacket back on the paper. Spread out the fabric, smoothing out any creases, and then draw around it to give a back shape. Pull out any gathers to take this fullness into consideration.

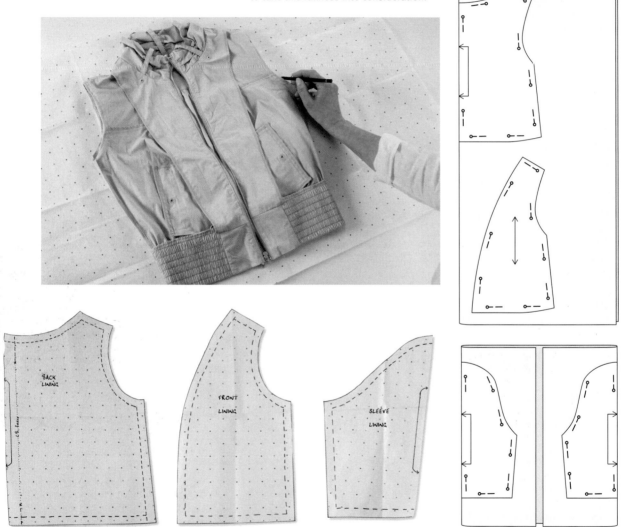

2 Cut around the back pattern and fold it down the centre back. Check the symmetry to ensure both sides are alike. Cut through the centre back and place one half on a second piece of paper. Add a seam allowance of 15mm (⅝in) round all sides. Add 2.5cm (1in) for a pleat at the centre back. When cutting out, place the back to a fold.

3 Repeat these steps for a jacket front and sleeve, adding a seam allowance to all edges. Trim the front edge of the jacket to allow for the facing. Make a pattern for half a sleeve – placing the sleeve pattern to a fold along its length. Make sure there is plenty of 'ease' to allow for movement and comfort within the jacket.

4 Fold the lining fabric in half and cut the back on the fold and two front pieces. On wider fabric, it may be possible to arrange the back and front pieces to make more economical use of the fabric. Refold the remaining fabric to the centre, giving two folded edges. Cut each sleeve to a fold.

5 With right sides facing, place the fronts and back together at the shoulder and side seams. Pin and then sew together. Trim and press the seams open. Insert the sleeve (see page 87).

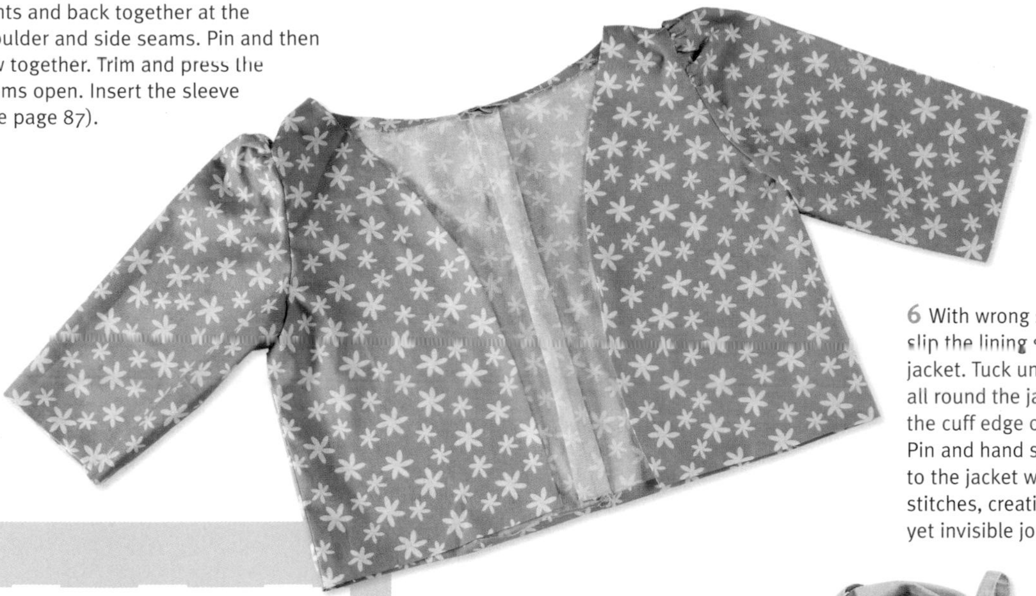

6 With wrong sides together, slip the lining sleeves into the jacket. Tuck under the edges all round the jacket and at the cuff edge of the sleeve. Pin and hand sew the lining to the jacket with tiny slip stitches, creating a strong yet invisible join.

TRY IT

(185) *Back pleat*

To make the back pleat, sew each end, securing with reverse stitches. With the longest straight stitch, join each end and then press open and flat. Remove the temporary stitches to reveal the pleat.

Temporary stitching

186

Lining a skirt

Making a lining for a skirt is easy, whether a commercial paper pattern includes one or not. A lining helps prevent the skirt from 'seating' (see pages 110–111) and makes it more comfortable to wear so that there is no need for a slip.

1 If making a skirt, cut it out in your chosen fabric and sew it together following the instructions given in the pattern envelope. This will include inserting the zip and completing seams, as well as creating any other style features. However, do not attach the waistband or waist facing.

2 Cut out the same pattern pieces for the skirt in lining fabric, apart from the waistband or waist facing. Sew together but instead of inserting a zip, leave a gap in the seam.

3 Slip the lining into the skirt with wrong sides together. Match up the seams and form tucks to remove excess fullness at the darts or pleats. Pin the waistband through the skirt and lining. Continue to construct the skirt, treating both layers as one.

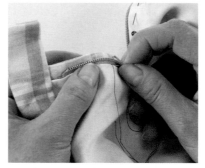

4 At the zip, tuck the lining seam allowance under and slip stitch the lining to the zip tape.

187

Skirt style variations

When lining a skirt, the method used will vary depending on the style. Adapt these suggestions to help when lining all sorts of skirts.

Straight

Leave the centre back seam open below the knee to increase stride length.

Tucks are made at dart positions.

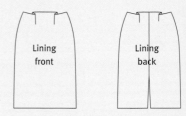

The seam is left open from knee level down.

Full gathered

The lining does not need as much fabric and fullness as the skirt. Gather the lining at the waist to match the skirt waist.

The skirt back has a centre seam.

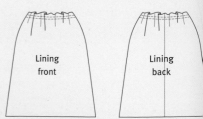

The lining is gathered to fit the waist and the finished lining hem sits 12mm (½in) above the skirt hem.

Pleated

Leave the centre front and centre back seams free below the knee to provide stride room. However, on a skirt with numerous pleats it is not necessary to have more than two seams with slits.

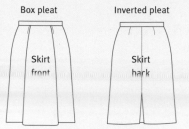

Box pleat   Inverted pleat

Tucks are made at dart positions.

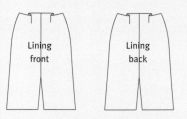

Centre front and centre back seams are left open below the knee.

A-line

For an A-line skirt, cut the lining the same as the skirt. There is no need to consider extra stride room.

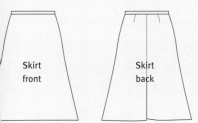

The skirt back has a centre seam and the tucks are made at dart positions.

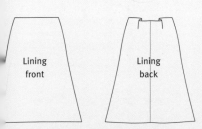

All lining hems finish about 12mm (½in) above the skirt length.

Underlinings

An underlining is an additional layer of material placed behind the fashion fabric to give extra body, warmth, density, support and weight to a garment or sewing project. It helps curtains to hang well and gives loosely woven fabric more support. Underlining can make an incredible difference to a completed garment.

Types of fabric for underlining

Many fabrics are suitable for use as underlining. Some are intended to be used on the inside and not seen, but it is just as appropriate to use fashion fabrics. Whatever you choose to use as an underlining, the additional layer beneath the outer shell will improve the finished appearance.

Silk organza

Perfect because of its strength and stiffness, silk organza is also very light and fine, and does not add unnecessary depth or weight.

Habotai silk

A bright colour behind a white or cream fine habotai silk can alter the shade of the top fabric, producing a more interesting finish.

Muslin

Muslin gives a bit of extra depth to a lightweight material and improves the hang.

Cotton lawn

Cotton lawn is lovely for adding extra weight and for improving the drape of a lighter fashion fabric.

Collar and cuff canvas

This very stiff interfacing, used in shirt making, is perfect for a corset or bodice. It gives a stiff, smooth finish that hides all ridges and wrinkles produced by the raw edges and seam allowances inside.

Iron-on interfacings

Modern fusible interfacing adheres easily and moves with the fashion fabric it is ironed to. This makes it an ideal way to add strength and support to whole garment pieces.

Tulle

Strong and resilient, tulle is great for keeping wedding dress skirts crease-free.

Needle-punched fleece

Sewn in between curtain fabric and lining, this thick layer improves the drape, aids insulation and keeps light out of a room.

FIX IT

188 *Is it possible to adapt a fabric that is too light or floppy for a suit?*

Cut a lightweight fusible interfacing in all pattern pieces and iron to the wrong side of the fashion fabric before constructing the suit. This gives a more substantial cloth but retains the desired colour and surface texture.

Iron a lightweight fusible interfacing to the wrong side of the fashion fabric.

190

Underlinings: the designers' best kept secret

Have you ever wondered why the top designers can justify charging so much for their garments? It is not just their famous name or their individual creations or short runs of a design, but the amount of effort that goes into each garment. In particular, their knowledge of how an underlining can transform a good outfit into a great one is crucial and its construction all takes time.

The addition of an extra layer of fabric mounted to the wrong side of the fashion fabric can alter the properties entirely. The choice of underlining will depend on the position on the garment and/or the finished look required. Once that decision is made, it takes time to cut the extra layer and mount it, by hand, to the wrong side of the outer fabric before continuing to make up the design.

Before underlining   After underlining

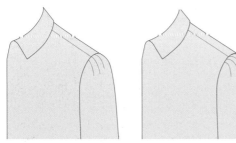

Before underlining   After underlining

Add body

If a fabric with a firm texture is used to underline a soft and limp fashion fabric it will help to keep the shape of the design. For example, a soft, silk blouse with a full sleeve may droop off the shoulder. With a silk organza underlining the sleeve head will retain its puffed shape.

Before underlining   After underlining

Add structure

If more than just a bit of body is needed, a collar and cuff canvas can be used to give a very firm finish. This is ideal for corsets and bodices, which will hold their shape on their own even without a figure inside them. Remove the seam allowances from the canvas, as it is too thick to stitch through, and sew it to a layer of cotton lawn. Mount this to the reverse of the fashion fabric, then sew the panels together adjacent to the canvas through the outer and cotton lawn layers. The advantage of this method of construction for velvets, beaded or delicate embroidered fabrics makes ironing unnecessary when the bodice is constructed.

Add density

Seams, facings and underwear will sometimes show through white and light-coloured clothing or those made from loosely woven fabrics. With the addition of an underlining in a more densely woven cloth (like cotton lawn), seams, facings and hems will all be hidden.

Before underlining   After underlining

Prevent 'seating'

Some straight skirts have a tendency to 'seat' through wear. Silk organza is a thin fabric made from highly spun yarn, making it a good option for underlining in this situation. It provides strength to support the skirt without adding weight or depth.

Prevent seam ridges

Pressing can sometimes emphasize a seam as the bulk of the seam allowances causes a shine or ridge along its length. By mounting an underlining to the underside of the fashion fabric, the seam allowances are further away from the surface and do not show up as much. Any fabric used as an underlining will help to prevent this problem and more than one layer can be used if necessary, provided they do not add unnecessary bulk.

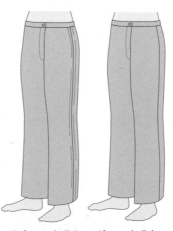

Before underlining   After underlining

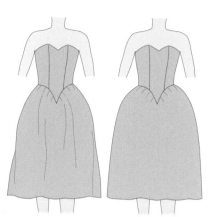

Before underlining   After underlining

Reduce creasing

Full skirts in certain fabrics can crease very badly when worn. Adding a stiff tulle or silk organza as a lower layer will help to keep the creases to a minimum as the stiffer underlayer stretches out the outer fashion fabric pushing out any creases.

Before underlining   After underlining

Provide a skeleton

To make hand stitches entirely invisible, add an underlining can be added so that facings can be anchored and the stitches of the hem can be sewn to the underlining rather than the dress fabric. This is particularly useful on satin, where the tiniest of hand stitches can be seen from a distance because the smooth satin surface is interrupted.

Underlining a skirt

Adding an underlining will help prevent the skirt from 'seating', especially if a loose-weave fashion fabric is chosen. The underlining supports the fabric and then a lining conceals all raw edges to give a perfect finish.

1 Cut the skirt panels in fashion fabric, silk organza and lining. Then set the lining aside.

2 Place the organza to the wrong side of the skirt front and pin around the edges.

3 Place a skirt panel on a table or ironing board with the fabric side facing up. Pin through both layers along the centre of the skirt. Allow one edge of the skirt panel to hang over the edge and separate the two layers with your fingers. Hand baste the seam allowance to hold the two layers where they lie naturally together. This makes sure that the underlining is fractionally smaller than the skirt, and the two layers will sit perfectly together when the skirt is completed. Repeat on all edges of all panels. Make up the skirt with the underlined panels.

4 Make up the lining pieces separately and drop into the skirt before attaching the waistband. This will conceal the underlined raw edges inside, making a beautifully finished garment.

Underlining curtains

Curtains with underlining hang beautifully, retain their shape, act as an insulator and keep the room dark.

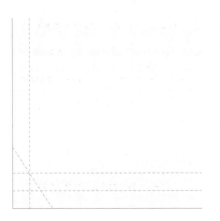

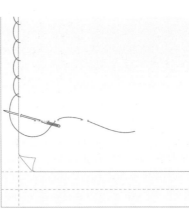

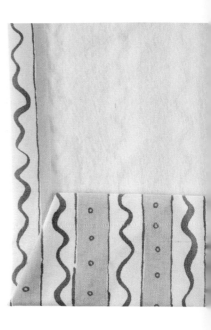

1 Press up the lower hem twice and the side hems once and unfold, revealing creases to use as guides to work to.

2 Cut the underlining to size and place to the side creases and upper hem crease. Trim the edge of the underlining so that it fits into the creases. Hand stitch with a lock stitch to secure the underlining to the creases.

3 Fold the side and lower hems into place, mitring the corner. Sew the side and lower hems to the underlining to secure them.

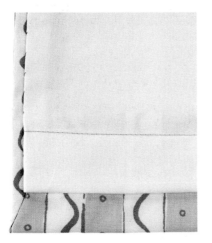

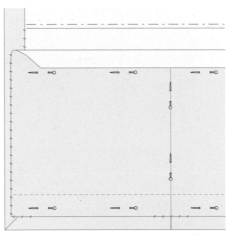

5 When the finished length of the curtain is determined, trim the underlining to the upper crease that is formed to reduce unnecessary bulk.

6 Fold the upper curtain hem down over the underlining and place the heading tape 3mm (⅛in) below this top edge. Tuck in the edge of the tape and machine stitch through all layers.

4 Hem the lining and place it over the underlined curtain with the wrong sides facing each other. Tuck in the side hems. Pin them and sew in place with slip stitches. Secure the lining to the hem at the vertical seams with a few slip stitches.

Interfacings

Interfacings, unlike underlinings, are used in smaller, selected areas and help to stiffen and support collars, cuffs, waists, yokes and facings.

193
Favourite interfacings

Traditional interfacings include hair canvas, linen and silk organza. Modern materials can be fused in place with a film of heat-sensitive glue on one side. These interfacings can move with the fashion fabric or provide more support and stability. Try several types on spare fabric to find the one most appropriate for each project you sew.

Hair canvas or linen

These woven interfacings are hand sewn into tailored jackets and coats to give shape and support to the collar and chest area.

Silk organza

Stiff and strong but without depth and weight, silk organza is ideal for supporting facings round necklines and front bands. It also helps anchor buttons and buttonholes.

Non-woven interfacing

The fibres in non-woven interfacings are bonded together like felt and do not have a grain or direction like woven fabric.

Available in a huge range of weights, they can be sewn or ironed in position. Use for collars, cuffs and facings, as well as for purses, bags and home furnishing projects.

Fusible woven interfacing

The latest generation of fusibles are constructed from woven polyester threads and have a heat-sensitive backing. Available in a range of weights, they work well with fine silks, synthetic fabrics and thicker woollen cloth. They can be fused directly to the wrong side of fabric panels. The interfacing moves with the fashion fabric so no edges are visible from the right side. Some have even been developed for two-way stretch fabric.

194
Applying interfacings

- As a general rule, select an interfacing that is lighter in weight than your fabric (unless making items such as valances).
- Use sew-in interfacing on fabrics such as velvet, metallics or corduroy and on sheer, delicate silks and silk-like fabrics. Pressing fusible interfacing could damage the outer fabric and is not advisable.
- Trim away any interfacing in the seam allowance to reduce bulk. This also makes ironing easier.
- When using fusibles, press carefully with a hot iron and press cloth. Lift the iron between pressings
- Always wait for fused pieces to cool completely before handling them. This helps the adhesive to stick firmly.

195
Interfacings for dressmaking and crafts

Iron-on fusibles

Fusible interfacings give speedy results, but use them only on fabrics that are suitable for hot ironing and steam pressing.

Super-light, iron-on

This is a fine, soft interfacing for lightweight, delicate fabrics such as rayon/viscose, silks, sheers and cottons.

Easy-fuse, ultra-soft

This comes in three weights: light, for delicate fabrics, cottons, polyester and soft jacket weights; medium, for gabardine, wool crêpe and linens; and heavy, to provide a structured look in suitings, coatings and heavyweight cotton blends.

Standard iron-on

This comes in two weights, both suitable for cottons and cotton blends. The weights provide different effects: medium gives the fabric a crisp feel and firm lends a stiff finish.

Sew-in

Always use sew-in interfacings with special fabrics such as those with beads or sequins; with pile fabrics, such as velvets and furs; and with fabrics that require a cool iron. Three weights are available: light, for delicate fabrics; medium, for heavier-weight fabrics, including velvets and furs; and heavy, for wool gabardine, tweeds and coat fabrics.

There are many interfacings available. Ask your local supplier for details of their full range to ensure you choose the right one for the job.

196

Interfacing a jacket

The type of interfacing chosen for jacket support is important but it is vital to apply it in the right places. The interfacing within a jacket should act like a hanger and not rely on the body to provide the support. This will ensure that uneven shoulders and hollow chests are disguised.

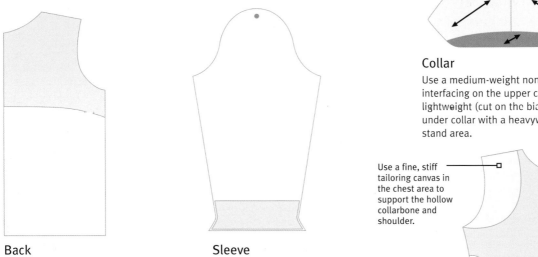

Collar

Use a medium-weight non-fusible interfacing on the upper collar and lightweight (cut on the bias) on the under collar with a heavyweight in the stand area.

Use a fine, stiff tailoring canvas in the chest area to support the hollow collarbone and shoulder.

Back

Use a medium-weight, fusible interfacing across the back, with a curved lower edge to move with the shoulders and support under the armhole.

Sleeve

Apply a medium-weight fusible interfacing at the cuff edge to strengthen and provide an anchor for stitches.

Front

Use a medium-weight, fusible interfacing, curved from the side seam and level with the back interfacing, down to the hem to support the front band and shoulders and not constrict the waist area.

FIX IT

 197

How do you avoid wrinkles when you iron on interfacing?

Unless the fabric and interfacing have both been preshrunk before being cut out, they will shrink with the heat and steam from the iron – and not at the same rate. To avoid this, place the fabric piece on the ironing board (wrong side up) and lay the fusible interfacing on top (glue side down). Hover the iron over the two fabrics, steaming without applying pressure. The fabric and interfacing may shrink before your eyes. Adjust the layers and, starting from the centre, lightly press the layers together. Lift and move the iron over the fabric piece until all areas are heated. Finally, smooth the iron over the fabric and interfacing to ensure they are fused firmly together. Allow to cool before continuing.

Facings

Use a lightweight non-fusible interfacing on all of the front facing to give additional support.

Perfect pockets

Pockets add a finishing touch to a garment, being both decorative and functional. Some people avoid adding pockets, worrying that they may make a mess of them and ruin the finished garment. In fact, a garment often looks more 'home-made' or 'cheap' without the addition of pockets.

198

Four

RULES FOR SEWING POCKETS

1 Anchor the pocket to the garment by adding interfacing on the wrong side to stabilize it. This will make the pocket stronger and support the shape of the garment: heavy keys or coins won't pull and distort the pocket and fabric.

2 Accurate positioning is essential. A patch or welt pocket placed slightly too far to the side or at slightly too much of an angle will ruin the appearance of a piece of clothing. Whether other people notice is not likely to be an issue; it is far more likely that you will always be aware of the flaw and therefore feel uncomfortable wearing the garment.

3 Stitching 'straight' is probably the most obvious concern. No matter how experienced and careful you are, when stitching is visible on the surface of a garment, that is the occasion the stitches wiggle or run off course. Take time to sew when topstitching and use an edge-stitch foot or guide to help to keep the stitching straight.

4 Securing the thread ends is vital for a pocket to be practical and remain firmly in place. As well as reverse stitching and tying off thread ends, it is a good idea to use bar tacks or stitch triangles at vulnerable points.

199

Patch pockets

This is probably the most obvious way to add a pocket to an item of clothing. It is cut separately and topstitched in position and is appropriate for all weights of cloth. Use patch pockets on jackets, shirts, skirts and the back of pants.

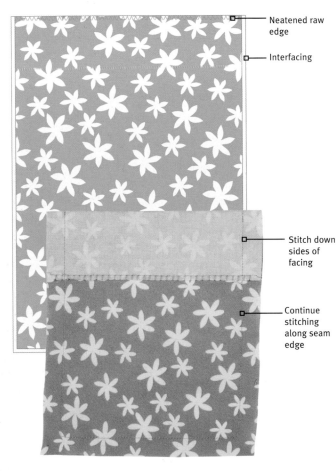

Neatened raw edge

Interfacing

Stitch down sides of facing

Continue stitching along seam edge

1 Cut out the pocket with seam allowances and any notches or dots to help with positioning. Having interfaced and neatened the raw edge, fold this top edge back on itself with the right sides together. Stitch the sides of this facing and continue along the seam line at the sides and base.

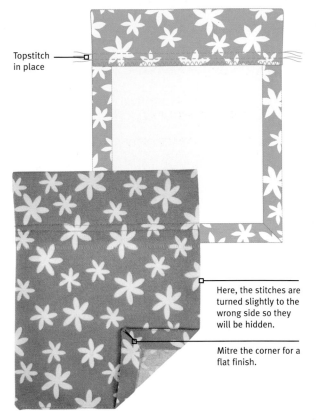

Topstitch in place

Here, the stitches are turned slightly to the wrong side so they will be hidden.

Mitre the corner for a flat finish.

2 Turn the whole pocket through the top-faced edge and press the seam allowance to the wrong side, mitring the corners. Topstitch to hold this faced edge down.

3 Pin and baste in place ready for stitching, then edge-stitch and topstitch the pocket in place. Reinforce the top corners of the pocket.

MAKE IT!

200 *Magic invisible patch pocket*

Although it is easy to sew a patch pocket with topstitching, a skilled tailor is able to sew patch pockets from inside, giving a more professional finish. Mock patch pockets have no visible topstitching but they are still securely sewn by machine, using a clever trick. Try it and amaze your friends with your skill!

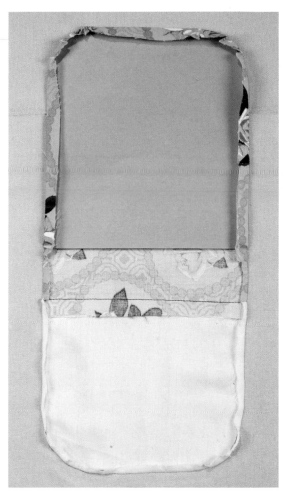

1 Cut out the pocket and lining, and join together at their upper edges. Cut out a card template of the pocket without seam allowances and place to the wrong side of the pocket lining. Draw around the card to give a sewing line guide. Position on the garment and stitch.

2 Trim all raw edges to a minimum and press the lining allowances towards the centre of the pocket. Place the card template to the wrong side of the pocket front and press the seam allowances over it.

3 Remove the card and pull the pocket front down over the lining, concealing all the raw edges beneath it. Pin, then slip stitch invisibly to hold the top pocket in place.

Use a small, fine needle for hand stitching and silk thread as it tends to knot and tangle less often.

201

Mock flap pocket

Sometimes a false pocket flap is a good choice when a functional pocket is not necessary and may well be inappropriate, spoiling the smooth line of a garment. Use mock flap pockets on jackets and dresses to add a feature to the style.

1 Interface the wrong side of the fabric at the pocket position. With right sides together, pin the front and back pocket flaps together and stitch on the seam line. Take a larger seam allowance on the top edge to ensure it will be hidden under the flap. Trim away excess seam allowance.

2 Turn through and iron the flap. Press the top edge seam allowance under, forming a crease to follow as a stitching guide. Finish with topstitching if necessary.

3 Place the pocket flap in position with the top of the flap facing the right side of the garment, but upside down. Pin and sew securely along the crease. Trim the seam allowance to 6mm (¼in). With a zigzag stitch, sew over the raw edge through all layers.

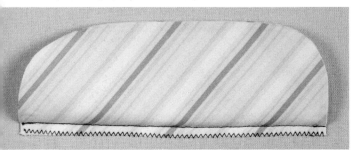

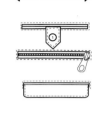

Various welt styles:

202

Pocket styles

Pockets primarily serve a utilitarian function, but also contribute to the look of a garment, so you should consider the look you want when choosing a pocket style.

Slant: Commonly seen on trousers made from all types of fabrics, from gabardine to jersey.
Curved: Similar to slant, and just as popular and versatile.
Curved and ticket: Widely used on jeans.
Kangaroo: Popular on the front of casual garments such as sweatshirt tops made from stretch jersey.
Bellows: A capacious gusseted pocket, providing a useful detail on coats, jackets, trousers and skirts.
Cargo: Derived from military wear and commonly seen on trousers and skirts.
Patch: Highly versatile and used on an array of garments including dresses, jackets, trousers and skirts.
Patch with flap: A flap on a basic patch pocket provides a tidy finish to the design detail of any garment.
Patch/welt: A double pocket detail that might be used for shirts and the inside pocket of tailored jeans.
Patch double: A practical and useful style, with one pocket layered directly on top of another.

Slant

Cargo

Curved and ticket

Curved

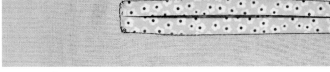

Bellows

Patch

Classic welt

Patch/welt

Breast

Patch with flap

Patch double

Welt pocket

A welt or jetted pocket is like an oversized bound buttonhole. This delicate pocket is finished with two narrow welts covering the opening of the pocket. Choose a welt pocket for jackets, ladies' blouses and trousers where a discreet pocket is required.

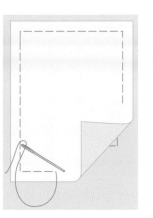

1 Interface the wrong side of the fabric support. Mark the position of the pocket opening as a long narrow rectangle by basting accurately onto the garment. Or, use a temporary marker on the wrong side of the fabric in the pocket position.

2 Cut a piece of fabric on the bias, about 20cm (8in) square and place this over the top of the pocket with right sides together. Pin or baste in place

3 Shorten the stitch length and, working from the wrong side, sew around the rectangle shape to show the welt position. Start and finish in the middle and not at a corner. Repeat for added strength if necessary.

4 Cut through the centre of the rectangle and up to the corners without snipping any threads. Once done, remove all basting threads.

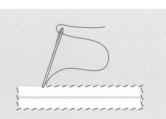

5 Pull the fabric square through the centre and manipulate the fabric over the edges pulling at the corners. Adjust and pin in the ditch so that the two edges are covered and the welts lie neatly. Prick stitch or stitch in the ditch to secure the welts in place along the edges of the pocket.

6 Cut a rectangle of lining fabric 8 x 10in (20 x 25cm) and sew each end of this to the edges extending from the welts.

7 Iron the pocket bag flat and manipulate the lining on the wrong side into position. Pin, then sew the side seams of the lining together and neaten appropriately.

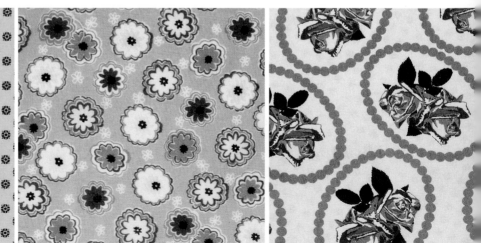

DECORATING FABRICS

Adding embellishments to a plain fabric or garment makes a design unique. Whether it is a wedding gown, bag, purse, T-shirt or cushion, the addition of threads, beads and ribbons add an attractive decoration to make it special. This chapter offers inspiration on ways to decorate garments and soft furnishing projects with 'how to' tips and 'make it' suggestions. Show your individual flair by decorating your own clothes and sewing projects.

Achieving quick effects

People who sew want their clothes to fit well and look special. Above all, they want to be confident that no one else will be wearing the same design. Elaborate embellished effects are not necessarily difficult and time-consuming. These tips for creating a special finish will save you time and allow you to concentrate your efforts on getting a perfect fit.

204 How can I achieve an individual look without hours of stitching?

Sew a simple sarong

When there is little time to sew before a vacation and you need a wrap or sarong for the beach, buy a length of brightly coloured fabric and just neaten the edges with a narrow double-folded hem (see page 95) or with a serger and a rolled hem (see page 97). This crinkle cotton fabric looks good, even when it has not been ironed – just wrap and tie as required.

Use embroidered or beaded fabric

Choose a simple shape but a highly decorated fabric for all or part of the design. Save highly decorative techniques and styles for plain fabrics.

Bold blocks of colour

Choose solid, primary colours for a child's T-shirt or coat and have different colours for the front, back and sleeves. You could even include a novelty print for very young children.

Lace

Team up a plain, simple dress with a lace jacket, wrap or shrug. The whole look could be in one colour, such as cream or white for a bride, or brightly patterned for an evening occasion. In both cases, the lace makes the outfit a bit more special.

Mixed zips

Choose a chunky zip for the front of a coat or jacket in a contrast colour for a bold effect, or buy two open-ended zips of the same type and length and then swap the halves to make a two-colour zip.

Beading

Beads, sequins and stones are applied to fabric for beautiful, rich effects on garments, bags, slippers and cushions. Although progress can be slow, a beaded design is a perfect way to make something unique and special. Use as a border on a collar, cuff or waist of a dress.

Organizing your materials is a great way to inspire creativity. Containers such as this partitioned clear plastic case serve to both organize and make your materials easily visible.

205 Beads, sequins and stones

Try embellishing your sewing projects with beads, sequins, or gemstones. Beads are generally symmetrical along a central axis, with a central hole through which you can thread; sequins are flat or cup-shaped with a small central hole suitable for hand sewing with short needles; stones are harder to sew on, but those that have been drilled, or those that have been 'claw-backed' (mounted with a metal fitting) are useful decorative extras.

207 Choosing beads and sequins

- Use glass beads if possible, as they will last longer and look better over time.

- When buying sequins, use price as a guide to help in your choice. The quality of the plastic used for sequins can vary; less expensive sequins may lose their colour or lustre.

- Choose beads of an appropriate weight or size for the design and the fabric.

- Test beads for colourfastness before sewing them in place. This will not be an issue for a hat or a purse that will not be laundered. However, the chemicals used for dry cleaning may affect the colour and lustre of beads or sequins on a jacket, for instance.

206 BEAD IDENTIFIER

Seed bead Also known as rocaille beads, seed beads come in many different sizes.	**Drop** These are narrow at one end and wide at the other.
Bugle bead Bugle beads are tubular in shape; they can be either perfectly cylindrical, made with flat sides, or what are called 'twisted' bugles. They come in various lengths.	**Cut bead** Similar in size to seed beads, cut beads have flat surfaces cut or moulded into the bead. 'Two cut' beads look like hexagons when viewed on the hole-side of the bead.
Flat-back These stones come in a variety of shapes and sizes. They have a flat, silvered back, and at least one hole drilled into the stone, making them an excellent embellishment for sewing onto fabric.	**Faceted** These beads can be round, roundel, drop or lozenge shapes, but are beads that have flat surfaces cut into them. The Swarovski brand is the finest example of cut beads.
Novelty A catch-all category that includes all fancy shapes, from leaves and flowers, to marquise, navette (boat) shape, stars and animals.	**Claw-back** These stones are not drilled, but set into a pronged metal mounting, which can be sewn into fabric.
Sequin These are round and either completely flat or slightly cupped with a hole punched in the centre.	**Lozenge** These beads are rectangular or diamond-shaped, with a hole drilled down the length of the bead.
Round These beads are spherical in shape – they can be glass, plastic or metal.	**Roundel** These beads are doughnut-shaped – they are made in plastic, glass, metal and rhinestone.

TRY IT

(208) *Do I have to create a garment especially for beading?*

If you want to try beading but do not wish to make a garment, buy something plain and add a beaded design to embellish it.

Beaded bra

Use bugle beads and seed beads to edge a plain bra. The scallops have five bugle beads and the drops in between are four seed beads long.

1 Trace a design onto silk organza and clamp the fabric into a hoop or frame. With a fine needle, sew beads onto the traced outline.

2 Make sure the beads are sewn securely on the wrong side and use a thread that matches the fabric not the beads so it will be less visible.

Beaded slippers

Decorate slippers with a rose design by tracing the outline onto organza stretched into a hoop. Sew beads to the organza and cut away the finished rose design. Hand sew the rose to the slipper, tucking the raw edges under.

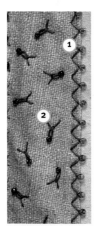

3 Trim around the outside of the finished design, taking care not to cut the beading threads. Tuck the raw organza edge under the beads to hide it.

4 Hand sew the beaded design into its final position with small secure stitches through the folded organza edge. Again, choose a thread that matches the fabric rather than the beads.

(209)

Adding beads to embroidery stitches

Small beads can be added to embroidery stitches as you work them. You will need to choose a needle to fit through the beads; so heavy threads are not suitable for tiny seed beads.

1 Work a line of fly stitches side by side, but before making the final holding stitch on each fly, thread a bead onto the needle.

2 This is a wheatear stitch. Before the final needle insertion, thread a bead onto the needle.

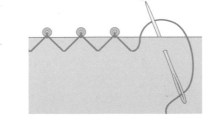

210
How do I stop my fabric from being pulled by the weight of the beads?

- Consider the backing fabric when choosing beads or stones. Large or heavy stones may drag on a light fabric, so try using smaller beads or sequins.

- Try giving the fabric extra support with an interfacing fused to the wrong side.

- Glass gems are generally lighter than genuine stones.

211
Carry a beading needle

Carry a beading needle with you when you are buying beads so you can test to see if they are large enough for the needle to pass through. There is nothing more frustrating than buying beads that are too small for the needle.

FIX IT

212 *How do I cut out beaded or sequined fabric?*

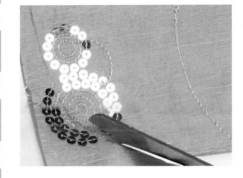

Cut out the pattern pieces carefully, avoiding beads and sequins which will damage scissor blades. Use a seam ripper or quick unpick to remove them. Keep them safely in a box or bag.

213 *How do I sew a seam in beaded or sequined fabric?*

1 Remove beads and sequins from the seam allowance. If there are too many, use a hammer to break the beads so that they fall away from the fabric. Fit a zipper foot to the sewing machine and join the fabric pieces together. The foot allows the needle to sew on the seam line without being hindered by the beads or sequins.

2 Finger press the seam open or, if the beads/sequins will not be damaged by the heat or steam of the iron, hover the iron over the seam to flatten it.

3 Using the beads or sequins saved at the start, hand sew them in place to fill any bald patches at the seam.

214

Applying beads, sequins and stones

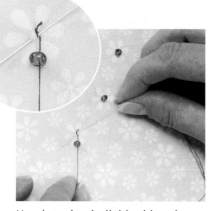

Hand sewing individual beads

The easiest way to sew beads and sequins to fabric is with a fine, long needle and strong, fine thread. Position them carefully and sew securely where required, finishing thread ends on the wrong side.

Sewing beads on a string (by hand)

Linear beads can be attached to fabric by hand or with a sewing machine. For hand sewing, catch the thread between each bead, holding it firm to the fabric with a second needle and thread.

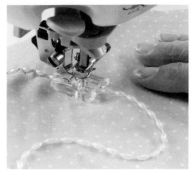

Sewing beads on a string (by machine)

Set the stitch to a long zigzag wide enough to cover the beads, and fit a beading foot. Place the beads over a guideline on the fabric and feed them under the presser foot so the needle can stitch them in place. The beading foot sits like a bridge over the beads, allowing them to pass through.

215

Tambour beadwork

Tambour beadwork involves a fine hook rather than a needle. Place the fabric in a hoop and pull it taut like a drum (hence the name 'tambour' from 'tambourine'). String the beads loosely and place them on the surface. The hook works from the wrong side, pulling the bead thread through the fabric and forming a chain stitch below.

3 On the wrong side, pull the thread loop through the previous loop and continue.

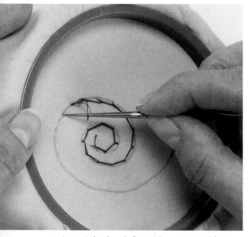

1 Insert the hook from the wrong side to the surface on the guideline.

2 Catch the thread between the next two beads and pull the thread back to the wrong side.

216

Sewing on sequins with beads

Sequins are metallic foil shapes with small holes punched for sewing onto fabric. They are often circular, but stars, flowers and other shapes are also available. If they are sewn on with small stitches in a similar way to beads, the stitches will be visible, even in closely matching thread. Another method is to sew them on with beads so that the stitches cannot be seen.

1 Choose a thread to match the bead. Secure the thread on the wrong side and bring the needle through to the surface of the work where required. Make a tiny backstitch on the surface, thread on a sequin, then thread on a tiny bead.

2 Take the needle back to the wrong side through the hole in the sequin. The sequin is secured by the bead, and the thread is hardly visible. Repeat the process of stitching through the bead and sequin for extra strength before securing the thread with another backstitch on the wrong side.

217

Sewing on shisha mirrors

These cute little mirrors with gilt borders are called 'shisha'. They come in two pieces: a mirrored disc and a stitchable, woven wire ring to hold each mirror in place. Originally from India, they add bold sparkle to any embroidery.

Choose a 100 per cent cotton sewing thread to match the border ring, such as yellow for gold rings and palest grey for silver. Thread a small, sharp needle and secure the thread with a small backstitch on the wrong side of the work. Hold the outer ring in place on the surface and bring the needle through just inside the outer edge. Stitch one third of the outer edge in place with tiny backstitches, then slip the mirror into place. Complete the stitching all around and secure the thread with backstitches on the wrong side of the fabric.

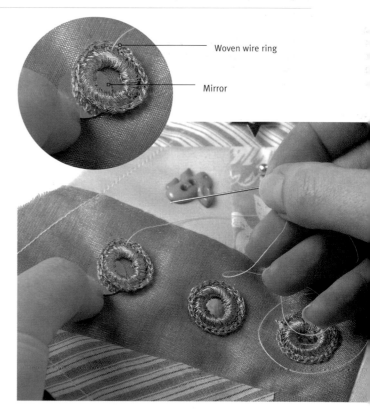

Woven wire ring

Mirror

218

Top tips for sewing beads and sequins

1 Use a fine, strong thread.
2 Choose either a natural (silk or cotton) or man-made thread like polyester. Polyester threads have a longer life.
3 Choose thread in a colour to match the fabric rather than a bead.
4 When sewing sequins, match the sequin colour rather than the fabric.
5 Use a long, fine beading needle for small beads.

Serger tucks are used to great effect in bridal pillows.

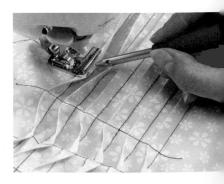

Twisted tucks and folds

You can create wonderful textured effects by tucking, tweaking and folding fabric to give it greater depth.

219

Types of tuck

Pin tucks

These tiny tucks are formed by stitching on the edge of a fold. The most important consideration with pin tucks is accurate measuring to ensure they are positioned carefully. To sew the tucks, set the sewing machine to straight stitch, iron a fold in the fabric and sew very close to the folded edge. This forms the ridge of the pin tuck.

Standard tucks

Tucks, and the spaces between them, may vary according to the look required. Measure the size of the tucks and the space between, then pin and press before stitching. To sew a standard tuck, feed the folded fabric under the presser foot and stitch parallel to the edge for the measured distance.

Serger tucks

One of the decorative effects created with a serger is tucks using the rolled hem stitch (see page 163). Simply set the serger for rolled hemming, disengage the blade, fold the fabric with wrong sides together and serge along the fold. Pull the fabric flat and the tuck sits like a ridge on the surface of the fabric. Use it for bridal pillows, camisoles, or as a pretty border on bed pillows and sheets.

Twisted tucks

The light shows off an interesting three-dimensional effect created by the moving folds in these twisted tucks. To make them, simply stitch over bands of standard tucks at regular intervals, twisting them back and forth to hold them down. Use a contrast thread to sew the tucks and twist them into place to make them more interesting.

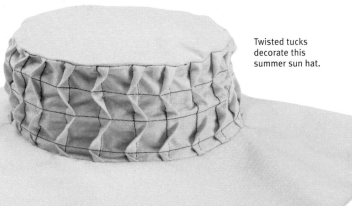

Twisted tucks decorate this summer sun hat.

Twin needle tucks

These are narrow tucks made on the sewing machine with a twin needle (two needles on one shaft). Two rows of stitching are created, linked with one bobbin thread on the wrong side. Greater depth is produced by adjusting the bobbin tension to pull the two lines of stitching together or by sewing over a cord.

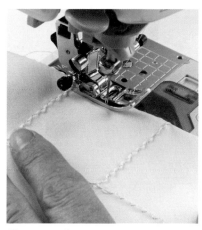

Zigzag tucks

A zigzag stitch gives a subtle but attractive finish to pin tucks. If a metallic or contrast colour thread is used, it enhances the effect. Set the sewing machine to a long and wide zigzag about 6mm (¼in) wide and 4mm (⅕in) long. Feed the fold of the fabric under the presser foot in the centre so that the needle swings to the right and left, catching the fabric on the left. The threads cross on the right and sit over the fold when the fabric is flattened out.

220

Top tuck tips

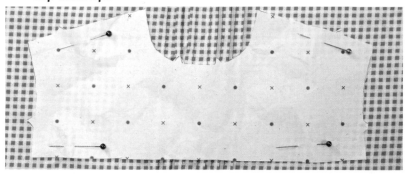

Tucks first

When making tucks on a panel for a garment (e.g. yoke) or soft furnishing project (e.g. pillow), make the tucks first and then cut the panel shape. This eliminates the need for complicated calculations and the chance of producing a panel of the wrong size.

Marking tucks

For perfectly regular tucks, mark them accurately before folding and arranging them. Choose a method to suit the project, the fabric and you.

• Vanishing pen
The marks made by these pens either disappear after a few days or are washed away with water. Always test them on a scrap of fabric first.

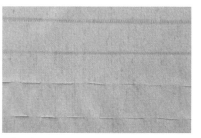

• Basting
Although more time-consuming, tuck positions can be transferred from a paper pattern to fabric with temporary stitches. Use a fine needle and basting thread to prevent damage to the fabric when the stitches are removed.

• Snips
If the tucks extend the whole length of the cloth, it is possible to mark with tiny 6mm (¼in) snips on the edge of the fabric. Keep the snips small and within the seam allowance.

Pressing folds

When the tucks are measured and marked, use an iron to crease the fabric. This helps to show the position of the tucks and makes them easier to sew. Remember, fabrics made from natural fibres crease better than synthetic ones, so choose cotton, linen or silk if possible.

Foot help

When sewing standard tucks, use the edge of the pressing foot as a guide to form a straight line parallel to the fold. Move the needle position to the right or left to achieve the correct width for the tuck.

MAKE IT!

221

Decorated evening purse

Make this little evening purse with a silk or satin fabric decorated with zigzag stitched pin tucks for added texture and interest. Or try a different type of tuck instead.

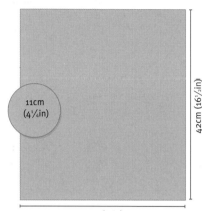

11cm (4¼in)

42cm (16½in)

35cm (14in)

2cm (¾in)

1 Cut a rectangle of fabric measuring 35 x 42cm (14 x 16½in) and a circle of fabric for the base with a diameter of 11cm (4¼in).

2 Mark and press even folds across the fabric every 2cm (¾in).

3 Set the sewing machine to a long and wide zigzag about 6mm (¼in) wide and 4mm (⅕in) long. Feed each fold of fabric under the presser foot in the centre so that the needle swings to the right and left, just catching the fabric on the left. The threads cross on the right and sit over the fold when the fabric is flattened out.

4 When the tucks are completed, place the side edges together with right sides facing and sew a plain seam. Neaten the raw edges and press the seam open. Pin the circular base to one end with the right sides together. Sew on the seam line to join the base to the sides. Trim and neaten the raw edges, then turn the bag to the right side.

5 Fold the opposite end to the inside, tuck the raw edge under and make a deep hem. Topstitch from the right side to hold the hem down, then sew a second, parallel line of stitching, 2cm (¾in) above this to form a channel. Unpick the seam stitches within the channel and feed a length of cord through.

Smocking

Traditional smocking is hand embroidery made over a base of tiny tucks. Used on farm labourers' smocks and children's clothing, machine-made smocking does not replace this skilful craft but is a quicker alternative.

(222)

Hand smocking

Stitch in rows to form a block of embroidery for yokes, cuffs and decorative bands. Prepare the fabric in tiny pleats (see page 133) and sew over each pleat with embroidery stitches. Use stem stitch and cable stitch as a firm edging to support the design; wave, trellis and diamond are decorative stitches used in the body of the work.

1 Treat each vertical tuck as a stitch. With the thread on the lower left of a tuck, make one horizontal stitch, taking the needle from right to left through the next tuck.

2 From the lower left, take the needle diagonally up to the next tuck, placing the needle through the tuck from right to left.

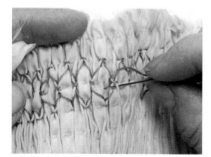

3 Make a horizontal stitch at the top with the needle inserted from right to left. Pull the two tucks together loosely.

4 Make the final stitch in the sequence by making a diagonal stitch down to the next tuck, taking the needle through from right to left as before. Continue with step 1 and repeat to complete the row.

TRY IT

(223)

How do I smock a child's dress?

Even a beginner can try simple smocking. Choose a diamond stitch (see left) and embroider several rows to form a block for the front of a child's dress. This saves learning several stitches and there is no need to follow a complex guide or pattern. The resulting work will have a more even tension than when several stitches are attempted at the start. Choose any suitable paper pattern, making sure the dress-front panel is cut to allow three times the amount of fabric to fit the yoke. This will give enough fabric to form tiny pleats for stitching on.

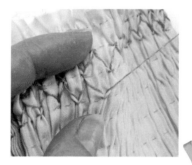

224 Machine smocking

1 Prepare the fabric in the same way as for hand smocking and support the back of the work with an adhesive stabilizer. The tiny tucks are then held firm and will not move when placed under the presser foot.

2 Choose an appropriate presser foot. Select one suitable for decorative stitching or use an open toe foot, which makes it easier to see the stitches being formed.

3 Select appropriate decorative machine stitches. Try these on a spare piece of fabric before selecting one you like. A triple stretch stitch or reinforcement stitch is a good imitation of cable stitch and forms a firm edge. Other possibilities include stitches that resemble a zigzag, fly stitch or cross-stitch. Choose stitches where the needle returns to the same position on more than one occasion, as this forms a double stitch that appears bolder, giving a stronger effect.

4 Having selected a range of stitches, sew rows of these across the pleated fabric. Use embroidery thread for the stitch with bobbin fill below. If the effect is too bland, use two threads in the needle for a bolder finish.

5 When the smocking is complete, trim away any loose threads and use the smocked panel as required in a pillow, bodice, purse, etc.

Prepare a rectangle of machine smocking, fold it in half and sew the side seams. Turn through to the right side. Add a flap, neaten the inside with a lining, and finish with a strap and beaded bauble.

MAKE IT!

225 Smocked pillow

Prepare a smocked panel for the centre and trim it to a regular shape. Balance this with two plain sections of the same size on either side. Cut a plain rectangle for the back of the pillow and finish with braid, cord, ribbon and/or tassels.

226

Perfectly prepared pleats

It is important to prepare the pleats accurately and to make even folds for stitching. The fabric can be prepared in different ways.

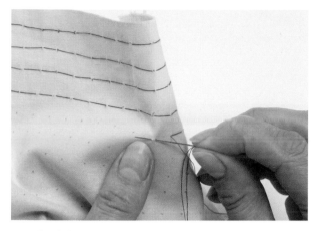

Hand pricking

Hand prick stitches in the rows and lines of a grid. These threads are pulled up to form the tucks.

Gathering by sewing machine

Using the longest straight stitch is not always successful. The threads form stitches on both sides of the work, which can hinder sewing the embroidery on the surface. Threads can also get caught under the smocking and the pleats tend not to be as even as hand pricking. Press a vertical line with the iron at one end of the pleating. Start each row of gathers with the needle in the crease to keep pleats straight and to prevent twisting.

227

Using a pleater

For anyone who enjoys smocking, a pleater is an essential tool as it reduces the time taken to prepare the pleats ready for embroidery. The row of evenly spaced needles penetrates the fabric while a crimped barrel feeds it through them in tiny pleats. The pleated fabric is eased from the needles onto the threads, which hold the pleats in place while the smocking is created. Although the process can be tricky, it is much quicker than marking out a grid of dots and then hand pricking each row to form the pleats.

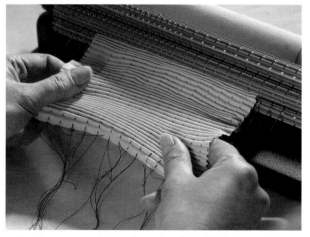

1 Thread up the row of needles with long lengths of thread. Roll the fabric onto the wooden dowel (barrel) and feed the front edge between the brass rollers at the back of the device. Turn the handle at the side to rotate the rollers which eases the fabric onto the bank of needles at the front.

2 Continue to turn the handle and work the fabric through the needles and onto the threads. Move the fabric along the threads and adjust it into neat and even pleats. When all the fabric has moved through the pleater, tie the threads at one end and pull up the fabric, adjusting the pleats accordingly. Secure the remaining thread ends to stabilize the pleats.

Quilting

This traditional craft has been used for bedding and clothing for many centuries. It joins two layers of fabric together, sandwiching a lofty filling with hand sewing or machine stitching.

(228)

Machine versus hand quilting

Personal preference dictates whether you choose to quilt by hand or by sewing machine. Quilting by hand is easier for some, as there is more control over where each individual stitch is made. Machine quilting is much faster, but can be hard work when a large quilt is being manipulated through the limited space on a sewing machine. Modern embroidery machines include some pretty quilt designs that are made in the hoop. Some models also offer a quilt stitch (three stitches forwards and one stitch back) as an alternative straight stitch, as it looks more like hand sewing.

TRY IT

(229) *Is there an easy way to try quilting?*

Use a walking foot and fit a guiding bar to ensure the rows of stitching are all parallel.

Make a bag with panels of quilting. Sew parallel rows of straight stitch through all layers to create the quilting and thus the bag.

Quilt around the outline of a shape on a printed fabric to highlight the design. Hand sew with a running stitch or use a machine straight stitch. If using the sewing machine, set the threads to automatically lock the first and last stitch, or leave long threads to finish off securely. This will prevent the stitching from unravelling.

230 Trapunto

In this style of quilting, smaller areas of the design are padded to give a three-dimensional effect.

1 Place muslin behind the quilt fabric and stitch the outline of the design through the two layers.

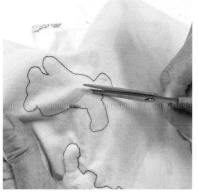

2 Where the design needs extra padding, cut a small slit in the backing fabric.

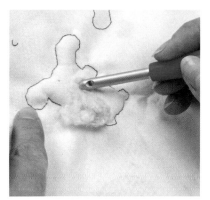

3 Stuff with soft filling.

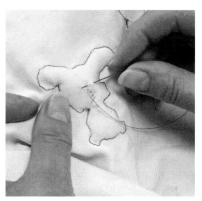

4 Hand stitch the fabric to close up the slit.

231 Quilting secrets

- Wash the backing fabric to preshrink it before adding it to your quilt.

- Unroll the batting and leave it for 24 hours before cutting it.

- Cut the backing of the quilt slightly larger than the front – about 5cm (2in) all around – otherwise the depth of the layers may cause the backing to pull in as it is stitched.

- When assembling your quilt, lay the backing fabric on a table (wrong side up) and smooth out any wrinkles. Tape it down with masking tape and place the batting on top. Flatten this and then hold it down with tape. Finally, place the quilt on top (face up), and tape again. Pin or baste the layers together and then remove all the masking tape.

- Pin the layers of a quilt together with rust-proof safety pins so they will not fall out. Specially shaped quilting safety pins are ideal.

- Pin or baste the quilt layers together, working from the centre outwards.

- Place safety pins in areas of printed fabric when working on patchwork. Any holes left by the needles will be less visible on printed cloth.

- Use a long needle when basting and stitching your quilt.

- Use a metal spoon under the point of the needle to make it easier to push it through the thick layers to the right side.

TRY IT

232 For corded quilting, thread a soft, loosely spun yarn through a channel formed by parallel rows of stitching.

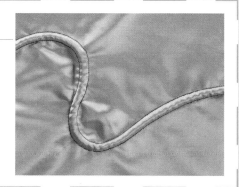

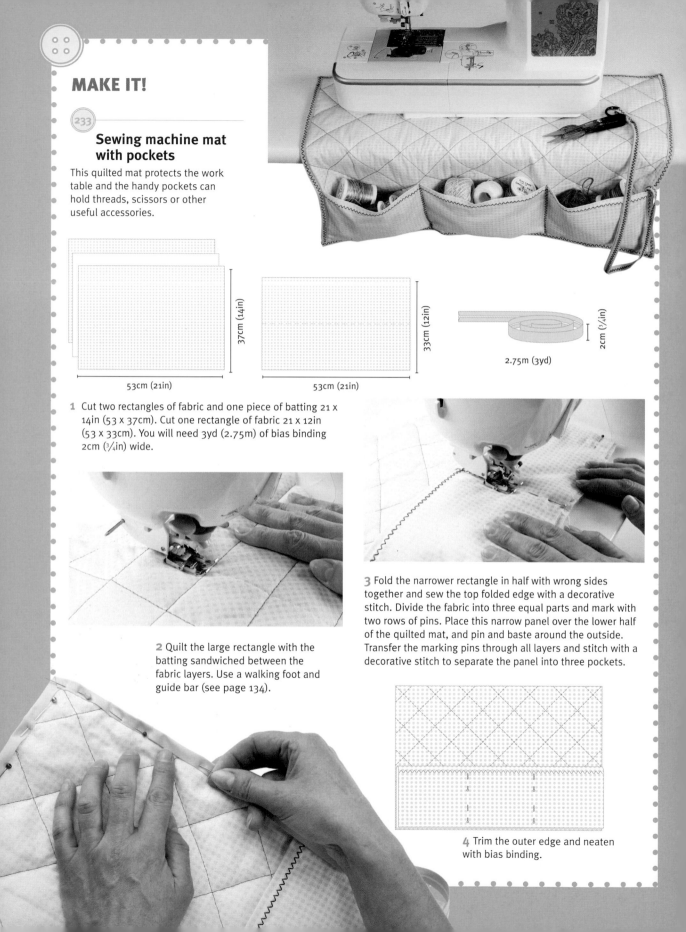

MAKE IT!

233

Sewing machine mat with pockets

This quilted mat protects the work table and the handy pockets can hold threads, scissors or other useful accessories.

37cm (14in)

53cm (21in)

33cm (12in)

53cm (21in)

2cm (¾in)

2.75m (3yd)

1 Cut two rectangles of fabric and one piece of batting 21 x 14in (53 x 37cm). Cut one rectangle of fabric 21 x 12in (53 x 33cm). You will need 3yd (2.75m) of bias binding 2cm (¾in) wide.

2 Quilt the large rectangle with the batting sandwiched between the fabric layers. Use a walking foot and guide bar (see page 134).

3 Fold the narrower rectangle in half with wrong sides together and sew the top folded edge with a decorative stitch. Divide the fabric into three equal parts and mark with two rows of pins. Place this narrow panel over the lower half of the quilted mat, and pin and baste around the outside. Transfer the marking pins through all layers and stitch with a decorative stitch to separate the panel into three pockets.

4 Trim the outer edge and neaten with bias binding.

FIX IT

(234) *Washing dilemmas*

Some embellishments can't be washed easily, so check for washability before you apply them to a project that will need to be washed. Non-washable embellishments are best kept for wall hangings, unless they are items you can temporarily remove, like badges. It is wise to preshrink braids and lace by soaking them in warm water first. Try a test wash for colourfastness before hand couching long lengths of braid. Hand-wash items decorated with buttons and beads, which may break in a washing machine.

(235)

Adding buttons, badges and baubles

Be imaginative and use interesting trimmings and accessories to adorn your quilted projects. Choose the trims to suit the colours in the fabrics and arrange them to enhance areas of the quilting. Beautiful buttons in all sorts of shapes, colours, sizes and materials can be sewn to your work to add detail and texture. Badges, brooches and other pieces of jewellery can be pinned or sewn in place too, after your hand work is completed. Keep a box to save interesting and unusual buttons and trims ready to use for these more creative quilt designs.

Buttons, beads and novelty trims work well with the embroidery on this patch-worked and quilted pillow.

Appliqué

As the name suggests, this technique involves applying fabric pieces to a backing cloth. It is a very versatile way of decorating fabric and some wonderful effects can be created. Use in patchwork or to decorate clothing and soft furnishing projects in styles to suit all generations and tastes.

Styles of sewing

Tucked under

Tuck the raw edges under and slip stitch the design to the backing.

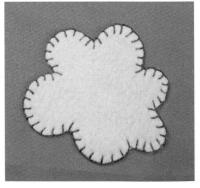

(237)

Top appliqué tips

• Stuck for ideas for shapes and templates? Look at a child's colouring book for simple and uncluttered outlines that are easily translated into appliqué designs.

• Decorating fabrics with appliqué can be a great way to get children interested in sewing. With iron-on adhesive film no basting is needed and the design is held secure while it is sewn in place. The results are quick to produce and look great.

• Where a design is not symmetrical and has a direction (e.g. lettering), make sure the outline will be facing the right way when cut out. If you are drawing the appliqué outline on the wrong side of the fabric or iron-on adhesive film, make sure the template is upside down.

Satin stitch (sewing machine)

Stitch a wide, close zigzag over the outline to cover the join between the fabric edge and the backing.

Pre-programmed stitch (sewing machine)

Select a blanket stitch, or another decorative stitch, and machine around the outer edge of the appliqué shape.

Blanket stitch (hand)

Leave the edge raw or tuck it under and finish with a hand-sewn blanket stitch.

238

How to hold appliqué shapes in place

Basting

This traditional method works well, but it is time-consuming and the basting threads can get stuck under the stitching, making them difficult to remove.

METHOD
- Cut out the appliqué shapes and position on the backing fabric.
- Baste the shape in position with a large running stitch.
- Machine with the selected stitch and then remove basting.

Temporary adhesive spray

Use this to hold appliqué designs in place while you sew them securely without the need for hand basting.

METHOD
- Cut out the appliqué design and place it, face down, on an old newspaper. Spray with adhesive glue, according to the manufacturer's instructions.
- While it is still damp and tacky, position the design carefully. Complete with selected stitching around the outer edge of the design.

Wonder Under (paper-backed fusible web)

This is ideal for flat appliqué. It holds the design to the fabric while it is sewn in place without the need for basting.

METHOD
- Iron the film to the wrong side of the fabric and draw the outline of the shape on the film.
- Cut out the shape, peel away the paper backing and iron it in place.
- Finish with the selected stitch and with no basting to remove.

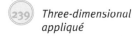

TRY IT

239   *Three-dimensional appliqué*

The three-dimensional quality of these red, pink and purple buttons look good enough to eat and the concentration of buttons provides impact and texture.

Cut around the berry shape and the sepals/stalk below. Finish all edges with satin stitch.

MAKE IT!

Appliqué wall pockets

Make the pockets on these wall hangings by folding down the top edge and topstitching in place, then pressing the seams to the wrong side. Decorate with appliqué, following the instructions below.

You will need:
- Two background pieces; one in fabric and one in very stiff interfacing
- Three pockets
- Two small curtain or lingerie rings
- Cord

1 Use novelty printed fabric and cut round suitable designs. Make the pockets by folding down the top edge and topstitching in place, then pressing the seams to the wrong side. Place a cut shape in the centre of each pocket.

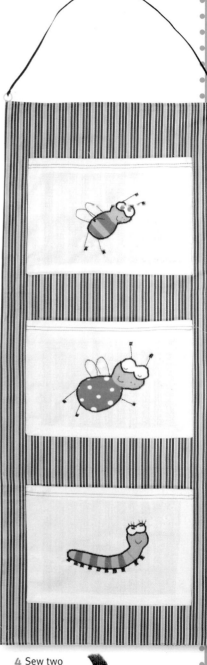

2 Sew round the novelty shape with a satin stitch to hold it to the pocket and highlight parts of the design with stitching.

3 Press the stiff interfacing to one of the backing pieces. Place the backing pieces together, with right sides facing, and sew round the outside, leaving the bottom unsewn for turning through. Trim, turn through, press flat and edge stitch to close. Mitre the bottom corners of the pockets and position on the backing. Topstitch them in place.

4 Sew two small rings to the top corners of the wall hanging. Tie cord to the rings and hang in place.

Couching

Heavy threads and cords, too broad to fit through a needle, can be sewn to the surface of fabric with overstitches. This 'couching' process holds the thicker yarns in place with hand sewing or machine zigzag. The cords are often sewn with an invisible or decorative thread.

Hand versus machine couching

Decorative knitting yarn, ribbon, gold cord, braids, metal plates, wires, and even strung beads and pearls can be attached to fabric with couching stitches sewn by hand or machine. For the covering threads – which secure the larger cords in place – use a clear or colour matching thread for an invisible hold, or a metallic thread for a sparkly finish.

Machine couching

When machine couching, use a beading or braiding foot, which feeds the cords through without obstruction, or an open-toe foot for finer or flatter cords.

Hand couching

Stitch the cords in place with tiny hand stitches. Use a clear thread for an invisible hold, a fine thread matching the cord's colour, or a metallic thread for a sparkly finish.

Couching with embroidery stitches

Many other embroidery stitches may be used to couch laid threads in place.

1 Turquoise ribbon, couched with blanket stitch.
2 Gold cord, couched with chain stitch.
3 White ribbon, couched with herringbone stitch.
4 Blue cord, couched with single cross stitch.
5 Turquoise knitting tape, couched with chevron stitch.
6 White ribbon, couched with groups of three French knots with tails.
7 Gold cord, couched with fly stitch.
8 Blue cord, couched with feathered chain stitch.

Silk ribbon embroidery

This embroidery is a great way to create a beautiful effect quickly. The ribbons are broader than embroidery threads, so fewer stitches are needed. The folds in the loosely sewn ribbons add depth and texture.

243
What needle should I use?

Choose a blunt tapestry needle with a large eye that holds the ribbon flat without creasing it. The needle must be broad enough to form a hole in the cloth to pull the ribbon through and it does not need a sharp point. Smaller embroidery needles will be required for finishing ribbon and thread ends. Cut the ribbon at an angle for easy threading.

244
Top ribbon tips

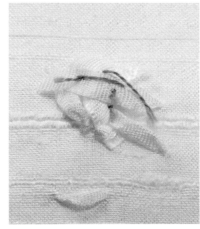

Securing thread ends
To reduce unnecessary bulk, start and finish the ends of the ribbon by stitching them to the wrong side of the fabric with a separate, smaller needle and silk thread.

Short lengths
Work with short lengths of ribbon, as the ribbons deteriorate slightly every time they pass through the fabric.

245

Four

**OF THE BEST MATERIALS
FOR SILK EMBROIDERY**

With so much on offer, it is often difficult to find the right material for the job. Read on to learn about the materials and equipment that is best suited to silk embroidery projects.

1 Fabrics

Loose and even weave fabrics, knitwear, T-shirting and even felt are ideal for silk ribbon embroidery as the ribbon can slide through the fabric without becoming damaged. Buy a ready-made hat or knitted jacket and try out the technique on the inside to see if it works before decorating it with flowers.

2 Ribbons

The best ribbons to sew with are 100 per cent silk without an edge or border. They are soft and twist beautifully, catching the light without having harsh edges. These ribbons are available in different widths for various effects. Some are suitable for narrow stems, leaves and petals, while others are better for larger flowers. Other ribbons like satin and organza can create pretty effects, but the softness of the 100 per cent non-edged ribbons cannot be surpassed.

3 Hoops

Hold the fabric taut in a hoop or frame while sewing. These vary in design but choose one of a suitable size that is comfortable to handle. The hoop or frame makes it easier to control each stitch as it is formed, allowing you to adjust until the stitch sits perfectly on the cloth.

4 Embroidery threads

Embroidery threads are often incorporated into silk ribbon pictures for stems, leaves and stamens. Choose cottons and silks in colours that work well with the design. Stranded embroidery floss is a good option as it can be divided and used in the number of strands necessary for the required effect.

MAKE IT!

246

Chrysanthemum

1 Make the main chrysanthemum flower first. Draw inner and outer circles as a guide for the centre of the flower and outer edge of the petals. Make petals between these guidelines with straight and some twisted stitches in shades of purple and lilac.
2 Form the centre of the flower with French knots in orange and brown threads to give texture.
3 Draw in the stems, bud and leaf positions with the temporary marker. Make the buds with straight stitch petals in lilac and cover the bottom half with loose, green straight stitches.
4 Complete the design in embroidery floss with stem stitch stems and satin stitch leaves.

You will need:
• Pale green cotton fabric
• 4mm silk ribbon in three shades of purple
• 4mm green silk ribbon
• Green embroidery thread for stems and leaves
• Brown and orange embroidery threads for the centre
• Darning needle for ribbon
• Embroidery needle for embroidery threads
• Temporary marker pen

Silk ribbon flowers

You can add silk ribbon flowers to knitwear, T-shirts, hats, pillows and bridal gowns. Here are some designs.

Ribbon stitch

Each stitch represents a petal. To make a single stitch, secure the ribbon on the wrong side and bring to the surface of the fabric. Loosely flatten the ribbon on the surface and take the needle through the ribbon and fabric near the end of the petal. Pull gently and adjust the petal with the back of the needle so it looks natural.

Ribbon stitch fuchsia

1 With 4mm purple ribbon, sew three long vertical petals.

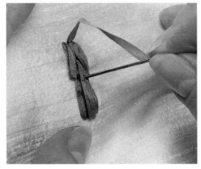

2 Sew five shorter petals over the first three, working from the outside to the centre.

3 Sew the calyx in pink ribbon in the same way as the rose petals. Finish with long straight stitches in embroidery threads and beads.

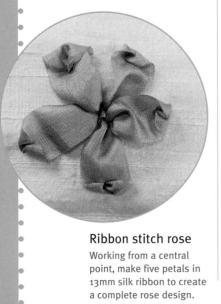

Ribbon stitch rose

Working from a central point, make five petals in 13mm silk ribbon to create a complete rose design.

Ribbon stitch leaves

Make leaves in various widths of green ribbon. Use ribbon stitches (like the rose petals) or twisted straight stitches, adjusting the length to suit.

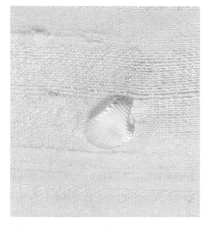

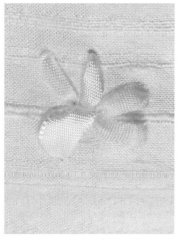

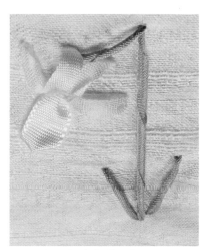

Ribbon stitch daffodil

1 In 4mm or 7mm yellow ribbon sew the trumpet with a short, loose straight stitch.

2 Sew four straight stitches above the yellow stitch in 4mm white silk ribbon.

3 Complete the daffodil with a green stem and leaves. Use 2mm ribbon and twist as you sew.

These periwinkle flowers are each made from five radiating straight stitches.

Ribbon stitch iris

1 Use 4mm silk ribbon and make a lazy daisy stitch for the upper petals.

3 Make the leaves and stems with long straight stitches in 2mm ribbon, twisting the ribbon to add texture. Add an embroidered stem.

2 Form the lower petals by making a stitch below and threading it behind the first petals.

Making tassels and fringes

Tassels and fringes are generally added for decoration rather than function. Use tassels on cords for tiebacks or on the corners of pillows. Use fringes on the leading edge or hem of curtains, on pillow edges, or on the hems of clothing. There is a plentiful supply of tassels in haderdashery and fabric shops but you can also make them at home. Simple examples require little skill, although more sophisticated tassels need more time and expertise. Fringes and braids can be bought or made at home.

MAKE IT!

248

Simple tassel

Make a simple tassel using some yarn and a piece of stiff card.

2 Thread a length of the yarn onto a tapestry needle and slide it under the wrapped yarn on one side of the card. Tie securely together.

3 Slide the wrapped yarn off the card and cut opposite the tied end.

1 Cut the card to the required tassel length. Wrap the yarn around the card until the desired fullness is reached.

4 Bind the neck of the tassel and secure the thread end inside so it is hidden. Trim the cut end to finish.

249 Tassel tips

- Use yarn or thread in a single shade, or mix colours or textures.

- Rayon and stranded cottons can be used for a smooth look and chenille or bulkier yarns for a more chunky tassel.

- For a perfect colour match, draw out threads from remnant fabric and use it to make tassels.

250 Finish with a fringe

Some loosely woven fabrics are ideally suited to fringing and finish a garment perfectly. Try this on a vest or a skirt.

1 Use shears to cut the edge neatly between two woven threads.

2 From spare fabric, remove a long, strong yarn and place it 2.5cm (1in) below the cut edge.

3 Set the sewing machine to a narrow zigzag (the width of the pulled yarn) and stitch over the yarn and fabric. Draw out all the threads above the stitched line. The zigzagged yarn will secure the edge and ensure that no more come out.

251 Adding a fringe

To make a fringed length for a curved edge to be inserted into a seam, cut a 4cm (1⅝ in) strip of fabric on the grain. Remove a band of 2.5cm (1in) of the threads from the weave on one side, leaving a 1.5cm (⅝ in) strip to sew into the seam allowance. Place this to the edge of the fabric and sew to the hem or into a seam.

For a frayed finish

On bias-cut fabric it is not possible to make a fringe by removing threads. However, an attractive edge finish can be created by deliberately distressing the bias-cut edge. Cut a skirt or dress to the length required and rub the threads on the cut edge with your fingers or nails. If the edge becomes too distressed and tatty after washing, it may be necessary to trim it to neaten.

Piping

Corded edges improve shape and outline. Use piping as a detail on pillows, slipcovers, bags and clothing. Use bought piping cords or make your own with self-fabric to insert into seams and edges to finish your sewing projects.

252 Buying piping cords

There are lots to choose from in a range of thicknesses. These cords have a flange attached, which allows them to be sewn into a seam. Trap the flange in the seam as you sew and the cord will sit securely on the outside edge.

253 Covering piping cords

Covering your own cord is simple. Select the thickness of the cord required and cover with bias strips of fabric to match or contrast with the project. Use fine piping for delicate edges on collars or cuffs, and thicker cords for soft furnishings.

FIX IT

254 How do I pipe corners?

The bias strips make piping flexible but additional snips and notches help achieve a neat finish. Pin up to the corner. Snip into the seam allowance at the corner position to release to the outer edge or flange. Continue to pin to the next corner and then repeat. Turn through. Pull and adjust the cording within its casing to remove wrinkles before finishing off.

How do I join cording neatly?

Overlap the edges and cut the piping edge to edge, leaving the bias strips. Wrap one end flat over the join and tuck the raw edge of the opposite end under before wrapping it over the lower layers. Trap within the seam to finish.

How do I cord with fine silk fabric?

The texture and twists in the cord may be visible through a thin fabric. In this case, cover with a bias strip of cotton lawn, then cover with a bias strip of the fashion fabric.

255
Top cording tip

Cord is available in polyester and in cotton. Polyester is strong and slightly stiff so it is ideal for soft furnishing projects. Cotton fibre cord is better for garment making as it is softer. Prewash both types before sewing to prevent it shrinking.

256
Can I decorate cording?

Create an individual corded edge by stitching over the cord with decorative thread before inserting it into a seam. Choose a stitch that covers the cording, such as a fancy zigzag. Metallic thread adds a subtle touch.

MAKE IT!

257
How to make corded edges

Cover your own cord and insert into vertical bodice seams, cuffs, collars, and waistbands or use to border pillows and slipcovers.

1 Select the appropriate thickness of cord for the project and measure the circumference.

4 Place the raw edge of the piping to the right side of the fabric with raw edges level. Stitch with a zipper foot.

2 Add two seam allowances at 1.5cm (⅝in) and cut bias strips this width. The bias strips lie smoothly around curves and corners. Strips cut on the straight grain will be more difficult to manipulate and will crease. Cut with a rotary cutter and ruler on a mat for an accurate and smooth edge.

3 Place the cord in the centre of the bias strip and fold the strip over the cord. Pin or baste (by hand or machine) along the length close to the cord.

5 Fit a zipper foot to the sewing machine to get close to the cord. Place the second layer of fabric over the cording with right sides facing and edges matching. Pin and baste through all layers. Turn over and sew from the opposite side. Keep inside the previous line of stitching to prevent these stitches showing on the right side.

Flower making

Flowers add a pretty finish to hats, purses and garments, especially bridal wear. Buy them in stores or make your own from fabrics and ribbons.

Shop-bought flowers make a lovely addition to a hat, scarf or hair accessory. Simply add a safety pin and attach.

(258)

Making fishing-line flowers

A serged fishing line edge makes the petals stand out and hold their shape. If you do not own a serger, set the sewing machine to zigzag stitch and try stitching over the fishing line and the fabric edge.

1 Cut a bias strip of fabric twice the required finished width and fold it in half. Set the serger to rolled hemming and thread with decorative embroidery floss in the upper looper. Cut a length of fishing line double the length of the strip of fabric. Feed the end of the fishing line under the needle and start to stitch over the line. Feed the raw fabric edges over the cord and continue stitching, allowing any excess fabric to be cut away so the stitches form over the fabric edge and fishing line. When the strip is completed, ease the line through the stitching to create a wavy edge.

2 Gather the folded edge of the strip with a line of running stitches and then roll up into a rose, stitching to hold the flower's shape.

(259)

Making fabric rose petals

Make a rose with individual petals to get a more lifelike flower.

1 Fuse two layers of fabric together with iron-on fusible film. Draw semicircular shapes on the joined fabrics and sew on the outline with a narrow satin stitch (see page 60). Trim close to the stitches.

2 Gather the straight lower edges with a running stitch and pull up. Sew the petals together in a flower formation, placing each over a gap in the petals below.

260 Making a fabric rose

Make these simple roses to decorate hats and bridal gowns.

1 Cut a bias strip 7.5cm (3in) wide by about 30cm (12in) long in fabric and in silk organza. Place the organza to the wrong side of the fabric and fold in half lengthwise, enclosing the organza.

2 Sew a row of running stitches close to the edges of the three raw sides and gather up.

3 Curl from one end and roll up to form a rose. Tuck in all raw edges and stitch together to keep the shape. Sew in position as required.

261 When to use flowers

- Use flowers to conceal problems! Add a row of fabric flowers to a bulky waist seam between a full gathered train and fitted bodice, or sew tiny flowers over cuts or marks on fabrics and add lots more to make it appear intentional.

- For bags and hats, consider fixing your fabric flowers in place with a hot glue gun rather than stitching them in place.

- When making fabric flowers and sewing them in place, use a double thickness of thread.

- Make flowers and sew a brooch pin or safety pin to the back and transfer them to different outfits.

Neatly folded silk ribbon forms the centre of this fabric flower.

262 Making a ribbon rose

Vary the size of the roses with your choice of ribbon and the amount you use. Narrow ribbons make small roses. A short length will make a bud, while a long length will make a fully opened rose.

1 To make a ribbon rose, fold in the ribbon at 45 degrees at both ends so that the raw edges are level with the base.

2 Thread a needle and make tiny tucks in the lower edge of the ribbon, starting from one end and working along the length, folding the ribbon as you go.

3 Make sure all raw ends are tucked to the inside and finish securely. Sew in place.

Silk flowers look good on silk garments and accessories, like this little bag.

TRY IT

263 *Colourful corsages*

Use scrap fabrics to create easy-to-make corsages. Cut a series of shapes from plain or printed fabrics in decreasing size order, and layer them one on top of the other. Finish with a bead, button, sequin or decorative machine stitch.

264

Suffolk puffs

Also known as 'yo-yos', these gathered circles were popular for making lightweight bedcovers in the early twentieth century. Their use as appliquéd texture makes them appealing for modern quilters or sewers.

1 Using a tailor's chalk and a scrap of fabric, draw around a circular object about 7.5cm (3in) in diameter.

2 Cut out the circles following the chalk lines.

3 Making a simple knot in the end of some sewing thread, make a running stitch around the edge of each circle and gather tight.

4 Make a few stitches in the gathered circle to keep the puff closed. Continue until you have enough puffs to complete your project.

265

Simple corsages

The edges on these flowers are left raw and unfinished. The petal shapes cut into the outer edges of the circles mean the edge is off grain at all times, so there is little chance of it fraying. This is a great project for children to enjoy.

1 Gather together some beads, sequins, fabrics, lace and ribbons in various textures and prints.

2 Cut circles in a range of sizes and trim into petal shapes around the edges. Iron with spray starch to stiffen.

3 Gather a circle in the centre of the fabric flowers and along the edge of the wider ribbons and lace. Pull up to form a circle.

4 Arrange the petals in size order, with the largest at the back and the smallest in the centre. Slip narrow ribbons, tied into large bows and loops of beads, between the layers. Sew the layers together through the middle. Decorate with sequins or beads in the centre and sew to a brooch pin at the back.

266

Bias binding blooms

The centre of each flower is sewn to secure it to a backing while the petals sit free on the surface. A single ring of petals sewn on a long stem, as shown here, gives the effect of sunflowers. A chrysanthemum can be created using many more petals in multiple layers with a smaller centre.

Try making a matching set of table mats, following the same flower design.

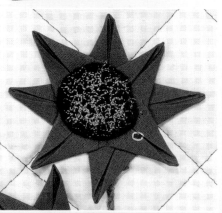

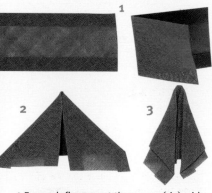

1 For each flower, cut the 2.5cm (1in) wide bias binding into eight lengths of 6mm (2.5in). Press the bias tape in half to form a central crease.

2 Form a point by pressing the top edges to the central crease.

3 Bring the outer edges to the central crease and press flat. It makes it easier to work with the petals if they are ironed into shape.

4 Arrange the petals round a central point on the backing fabric and baste in place.

5 Cut a circle of felt to cover the raw edges in the middle of the petals and baste in place. Drop the feed dogs and fit a darning foot to the sewing machine. Then, using free machine embroidery, sew the centre of the flower.

Glossary

Appliqué: where a piece of fabric is sewn to a base material to create a decorative effect.

Balance points: balance points or marks refer to all notches and dots that help to align fabric pieces when constructing a garment.

Bar tacks: a short block of satin stitches that strengthen a stress point, often used on a pocket.

Basting (tacking): temporary stitching by hand or machine.

Batting: used in quilting, this material is a thick soft layer of insulation sitting between the surface fabric and backing layer. It is also known as wadding.

Couching: a method where heavy, thick threads or cords are applied to the surface of a fabric.

Fabric: the result of yarns having been woven or knitted together. In some cases, fibres are felted or bonded direct into fabric.

Feed dogs: these teeth lie under the presser foot and move the fabric to allow the needle to make each stitch.

Fibre: refers to a single natural or synthetic 'hair' which is then spun with others into a yarn.

Finger pressing: when using an iron is not appropriate, fingers can push fabric into place.

Interfacing: a stabilizing fabric placed to the inside of a garment to add support. Used in small areas like the collar or cuffs.

Layering (grading): when trimming raw edges to limit bulk on the inside, trim each layer to a different height.

Lining: a separate fabric sewn on the inside of a garment to hide all the raw edges and make it hang well.

Muslin: a test or mock up of a garment made in a cheap cloth. In the UK this is referred to as a 'toile'.

Nap: this refers to a surface texture on a cloth that makes it appear different from different angles. Pattern pieces must be cut in the same direction on a napped fabric.

Notions: the items required to complete a garment or project including zips, buttons, elastic, etc.

Patchwork: where small pieces of fabric are arranged and joined together to form larger designs. Used for quilts, clothing, and home décor projects.

Pattern markings: symbols in the form of dots, triangles and arrows giving information to help with cutting and joining fabric pieces.

Pile: refers to extra fibres or loops that have been woven or knitted into a fabric during manufacture. E.g. velvet or towelling.

Pilling: through wear, some small balls of fibre appear on the surface of some synthetic fabrics. They can be picked or cut off.

Point press and basher: a hard wood tool used to get to difficult-to-access areas when pressing tailored garments and for flattening jacket edges and collars.

Princess line: a dress with curved seaming running from the shoulder or armhole to the hem on the front and back, giving six panels (not including the centre back seam).

Seam allowance: the area between the sewing line and the edge of the cloth normally 1.5cm (⅝in) but 2.5cm (1in) in couture sewing.

Selvedge: the finished edges of a cloth that do not ravel.

Serger: a machine designed to sew and finish edges in one step although it can produce many other effects too. Also called an overlocker.

Smocking: embroidery sewn on a base of tiny tucks or folds.

Spi: or stitches per inch. An alternative to using millimetres to describe stitch length.

Stay stitch: stitching used to hold fabric stable and prevent it from stretching when sewing seams.

'Stitch in the Ditch': a term used where pieces are held together by stitching on the right side of a previously made seam, e.g. on a waistband.

Stitch triangles: a triangle of stitches made at the corners of the opening of a patch pocket to strengthen the stress points.

Tambour: a type of beadwork using a hook rather than a needle.

Tailor's dummy (or dress form): is a mannequin used to assist fitting when making garments.

Tailor's ham: a hard, ham-shaped cushion, traditionally filled with sawdust, used as a pressing aid.

Toile: a trial or mockup of a garment to check the fit before a finished garment is constructed. In the US, this is referred to as 'muslin'.

Trapunto: a type of quilting.

Underlining (interlining): where an entire panel in a garment is backed by a second layer of fabric to add body and support.

Under stitch
This is when the seam allowances are stitched to the wrong side of a garment and the stitching in not seen on the right side, e.g. on an armhole facing.

Yarn: when fibres are spun together, they make yarn.

Resources

Patterns and threads

www.madeirausa.com
www.simplicitynewlook.com
www.voguepatterns.com
www.mccall.com
www.butterick.com
www.sewingpatterns.com

Sewing machines

www.brother.com
www.babylock.com
www.husqvarnaviking.com
www.berninausa.com
www.elena.com
www.janome.com
www.pfaff.com
www.singer.com

Smocking Pleater

House of Smocking www.smocking.co.uk

Interfacing products

English Couture Company
The Swan Centre
8A Swan Street
Sileby
Leicestershire
LE12 7NW
01509 813186

Vilene Interlinings
Lowfields Business Park
Elland
West Yorkshire
HX5 9DX
01422 32 7900

Fabrics

Rowan Yarns
Green Lane Mill
Holmfirth
West Yorkshire
England
HD9 2DX
www.knitrowan.com

Magazines

Threads Magazine
www.taunton.com/threads

Sewing World Magazine
www.sewingworldmagazine.com

Sew Today
www.sewtoday.co.uk

Sew Magazine
www.sewmag.co.uk

Vogue Patterns
www.voguepatterns.com

Useful sewing sites

Hints and tips and news of events
www.isew.co.uk

The chance to exchange sewing questions and advice
www.thesewingforum.co.uk

Recommended reads

Bible of Sewing Techniques for Home Décor
by Julia Bunting
Search Press, 2009

Compendium of Quilting Techniques
by Susan Briscoe
Search Press, 2009

The Encyclopedia of Sewing Techniques
by Susan Briscoe
Search Press, 2003

Index